# LOVE THE QUESTIONS

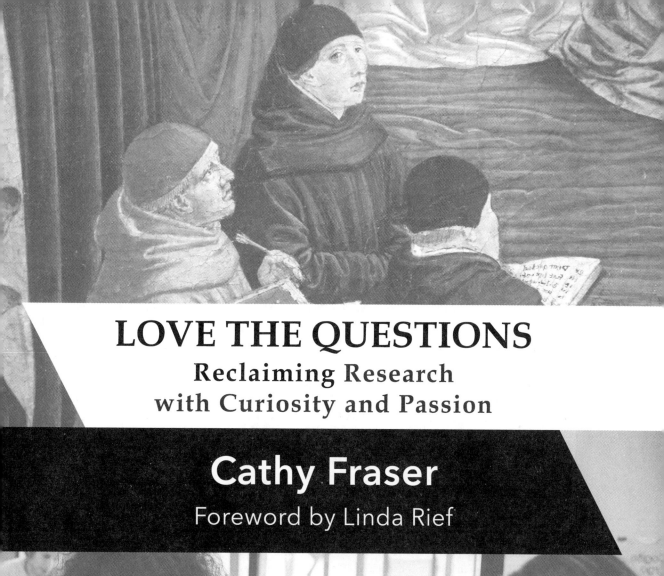

# LOVE THE QUESTIONS
### Reclaiming Research
### with Curiosity and Passion

## Cathy Fraser
Foreword by Linda Rief

**Stenhouse Publishers**

Portsmouth,
New Hampshire

# Stenhouse Publishers

www.stenhouse.com

Credits

Figure 2.2: Photo of Halyard Sterling Nitrile Powder-Free Exam Gloves used with permission of Halyard Health.

Figure 7.1: Screenshot of zapatopi.net/treeoctopus/ reprinted with permission of Lyle Zapato, zapatopi.net.

Appendix A: *A Teacher's Guide to the Multigenre Research Project: Everything You Need to Get Started* by Melinda Putz. Copyright © 2006 by Melinda Putz. Published by Heinemann, Portsmouth, NH. Reprinted by permission of the Publisher. All Rights Reserved. From *The Multigenre Research Paper: Voice, Passion, and Discovery in Grades 4–6* by Camille A. Allen. Copyright © 2001 by Camille A. Allen. Published by Heinemann, Portsmouth, NH. Reprinted by permission of the Publisher. All Rights Reserved.

Library of Congress Cataloging-in-Publication Data

Names: Fraser, Catherine A., 1965- author.
Title: Love the questions: reclaiming research with curiosity and passion / Catherine A. Fraser.
Description: Portland, Maine: Stenhouse Publishers, [2018] | Includes bibliographical references and index.
Identifiers: LCCN 2018024813 (print) | LCCN 2018044090 (ebook) | ISBN 9781625311993 (ebook) | ISBN 9781625311986 (pbk. : alk. paper)
Subjects: LCSH: Research--Study and teaching (Elementary) | Research--Study and teaching (Secondary) | Report writing--Study and teaching (Secondary) | Report writing--Study and teaching (Elementary) | Information literacy--Study and teaching (Elementary) | Information literacy--Study and teaching (Secondary)
Classification: LCC LB1047.3 (ebook) | LCC LB1047.3 .F8125 2018 (print) | DDC 370.72--dc23
LC record available at https://lccn.loc.gov/2018024813

Cover and interior design by Lucian Burg, LU Design Studios, Portland, ME
www.ludesignstudios.com

Manufactured in the United States of America

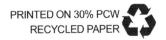

PRINTED ON 30% PCW
RECYCLED PAPER

24 23 22 21 20 19 18       9 8 7 6 5 4 3 2 1

# Dedication

To Wayne, who supports me in all things,

and to Sarah and Laura, who amaze and inspire me

# Contents

# Foreword

*Research—the intense pursuit of answers—should occupy one's waking hours. It should pop up in one's thoughts at odd times of the night. It should prickle the intellect as a persistent itch prickles the skin. It should be a passion, a temporary obsession, page count unlimited. It should not be a pesky, tedious assignment.*

—Cathy Fraser

This was the first of five pages of notes I copied down from Cathy's book as I read her manuscript. *Yes,* I thought, *this is exactly what I hope my students are thinking when they hear the word* research. (I can hear your laughter, thinking about your students as I say that.)

Unfortunately, I know better. We all know better. Whether from previous experiences of being given a topic, given a format (five paragraphs that include the thesis statement and a conclusion that repeats the statement), given little time to search out information, or given only Google as a resource, this is far from what many students think as the word *research* echoes through their brains and leaves them numb with anticipated boredom. The word conjures everything that is bad about writing: no choice, no time, no interest, no direction.

Here are the only questions that "prickle their intellect" when the *research* word is mentioned: *What's the topic? How long does it have to be? When's it due?*

I hope I have turned my students' thinking around by guiding them to learn more about what they are already passionate or curious about. Their topics come from them. The length is as long as it has to be to say what they need to say. And due dates are dictated by the time it takes to gather and shape information, within a reasonable time frame.

Yes, I have tried to turn my students' thinking toward writing about those topics or issues that matter to them, even in research. Especially in research. In this book, I have learned much more from Cathy. Thus, the five pages of notes. Here is just some of what I've learned:

- How to find topics out of curiosity and interest
- How to look for resources well beyond Google
- How to take notes from a complex informational source
- How to make that information relevant and personal, instead of plagiarizing someone else's thinking
- How to talk to writers in the process of locating information and writing about their discoveries
- How to use a multigenre approach to the framing of findings
- How to reflect on the research by thinking through the process that led to the findings

Perhaps most important, Cathy asks and answers the question *Why does assigning research matter?* As with anything we ask our students to try, we should know and understand *why* we are asking them to do this work. What is there to gain? Will this help our students grow as readers and writers, as well as become active participants in a democratic society? Cathy says:

> Kids must learn how to ask probing questions, find information—the good stuff—analyze situations logically, and create solutions.
>
> I don't say that lightly.
>
> Self-advocacy, agency, confidence in decision making—these are all by-products and benefits of research skills. Citizens who educate themselves, who can broaden and narrow subject matter, who develop awareness of when more information is needed, who question, read closely, spot and form argument, analyze, make connections, and synthesize are good citizens indeed.

Cathy takes us and our students where we need to go, showing us how to get there and why it matters, in the hopes that they are kept awake at night by the intense pursuit of answers and not because something is a "pesky assignment."

This book is especially important to me. Four years ago, Ryan Gilpatrick, assistant principal, and a group of teachers—one of whom was Cathy—at Prospect Mountain High School in Alton, New Hampshire, asked me if I would consider facilitating a monthly workshop for teachers focused on writing. Language arts, history, science, art, and math teachers were all interested in finding ways to make their students' writing better. One year turned into three years—2014 through 2017. The teachers wrote. Then they took their ideas and their discoveries about writing into their classrooms.

In faculty meetings, the teachers in the writing group took the staff through much of the writing they had done, sharing the processes for finding writing, giving students choice about what they wrote, giving feedback that moved the writing forward, connecting the writing to a variety of disciplines by using mentor texts as models, and asking students to reflect on the process they went through.

During the time that we met, two-and-a-half hours once a month for ten months each year, I asked the teachers to write at least one personal piece and one professional piece. Cathy's professional piece always went back to helping students find ways to research topics and issues in relevant ways. The writing she was doing was never finished. It was always growing and changing. She read books and articles. She talked to librarians, teachers, university professors, and students. She drafted and redrafted. She sought out feedback. She lay awake at night trying to figure out what was working, what wasn't. She redesigned research courses she taught at the high school. She sent me e-mails asking more questions, sharing more thinking and discoveries. We often talked on the way to our cars after those writing workshops, standing in the dark in the parking lot of the high school, car doors open, probing each other with questions and wonderings.

What I especially love about this book is that Cathy has found a way to weave in personal stories that show her humanity, make her real, and reflect on the research process. Through reading this book I know Cathy better, and I know how to help my students find research topics that matter enough to them that they will persist with the process.

Sometimes Cathy's confidence wavered, but she had the patience and the tenacity to stick with the very hard work of research and writing that had become her obsession. This book is the result of years of research. It is a mentor text into the entire research process.

I am so proud of her and all of the teachers at Prospect Mountain who wrote, rewrote, and wrote more. We laughed. We cried. We talked. We saw each other as learners whose writing touched us intellectually and emotionally. We began to know one another. Their stories, their questions, their thinking, and their writing have made the writing of their students much stronger. I am humbled to have been a part of the process with all of these teachers, as well as with Cathy and the writing of this book. I remember writing on one of the sticky notes as I responded to a draft of her thinking: "You know, you have a book in you that needs to be shared with others."

Indeed. Her book has come to be.

Linda Rief teaches and learns at Oyster River Middle School in Durham, New Hampshire. She is also an instructor at the University of New Hampshire Summer Literacy Institute. She is the author of *The Quickwrite Handbook* (2018), *Read Write Teach* (2014), and *Inside the Writer's-Reader's Notebook* (2007), and coeditor with Kylene Beers and Robert Probst of *Adolescent Literacy* (2007), all published through Heinemann Publishers.

# Acknowledgments

First, I must acknowledge the administrators at Prospect Mountain High School, Mr. J Fitzpatrick and Mr. Ryan Gilpatrick, whose foresight and commitment to continuous improvement brought Linda Rief to us. Without that course of events and Linda's influence, this book would not exist. Linda, I owe you a great debt of gratitude for your work, encouragement, and coaching, and for making yourself accessible. Thank you so much.

Thank you, Chris Reeves, who served as a sounding board throughout this entire project, tirelessly reading chapters and making expert suggestions. Couldn't have done this without you.

Next, I would like to acknowledge Tom Newkirk, who encouraged me to have the confidence to persevere. Thank you for your work, Tom. The Literacy Institute classes and keynote addresses you've delivered that I've been fortunate enough to attend and benefit from, as well as your many books, have informed my practice more than you will ever know.

Finally, thank you to Stenhouse Publishers for believing in this project, especially Maureen Barbieri, Grace Makley, and the production crew, who fine-tuned the writing and presentation of the material in these pages. Maureen, you have the patience of a saint!

# Introduction

I f you ever want to see what real research looks like, watch a *Law & Order* episode. To open, a crime has been committed and discovered. Evidence from the scene has been collected, cataloged, and/or sent for analysis. Detectives assigned to the case, using the evidence at hand, start visiting and questioning witnesses. They read phone records and follow Internet trails. Witnesses either obfuscate or come clean. Sometimes they point detectives to other witnesses. Questions abound: *Who did it? How? Why?* In particularly puzzling cases we see detectives theorizing with colleagues as they pore over evidence in the station room. There are setbacks. Witnesses close to the perpetrator "get dead" sometimes, raising even more questions. DNA evidence can be inconclusive or point detectives in a totally different direction, causing them to revisit the scene and/or some of the witnesses, or to reexamine collected data with a perspective not previously considered. Detectives work their theories until they can practically reconstruct the events leading up to the crime. Data collected must be handled carefully and remain sacrosanct. This series is formulaic, but we can't tear ourselves away because we are fascinated, appalled, and intrigued all at the same time.

All the parts of the research process are there: defining the task, locating and accessing information, using and evaluating the information, synthesizing, and reflecting (Eisenberg and Berkowitz 2000). As detectives acquire more background knowledge, more questions are raised, which leads them either to locate and analyze more information or to revisit the data they collected and view it through a different lens. At the end, there are almost always unanswered questions. When we see this process played out, we discover that research is not linear but recursive.

Loose threads, unsolved mysteries—these bother us like an itch we need to scratch. We follow the thread to see where, or if, it ends. Some of us devote our whole lives to the pursuit of new knowledge.

This picture of research differs greatly from the assignments students complete for school, where they are compelled to work through a series of tasks that begins with selecting a topic from a teacher-generated list and culminates in a written report. There is no question to answer or intrigue to pursue, save for those provided by the teacher to stimulate writing on content in the discipline.

All sources consulted must be properly documented using an academic citation format. Maybe one of the sources must be a print one. Maybe there must be three sources used at a minimum. Paper: 3–5 pages; PowerPoint: 7–10 slides; Oral Presentation: 5–8 minutes.

Within this discrete structure there is no room for theorizing. Data collected are irrefutable and unalterable facts. Any questions posed originate from the teacher. There is no real analysis needed, because the information is portable and can't be changed. There's no opportunity for students to turn things over in their minds; the project duration from start to finish is typically one to two weeks. There must be a citation at the end of every paragraph, or on every slide, because there are no original thoughts emanating from the student—which is actually plagiarism.

Students tend to dread research projects. Under these circumstances, who can blame them?

In the fall of 2015, I conducted a small, informal survey that eventually led to a larger research study. The participants in my survey came from two college preparatory science classes composed of sophomore students. The classes were heterogeneously grouped to include traditional college-prep students along with students who would filter out to honors level as juniors. The survey included a dozen questions, all focused on students' perceptions of their individual research processes; these ranged from how they decide on topics to how much time they put into thinking and reading about the topic to how much time they typically have to complete the project. The responses were indicative of prevailing trends and attitudes toward research on the secondary level, and they validated what I've observed in my practice.

Seventy-one percent of the students surveyed indicated that they have little choice in research topics, saying that the teacher usually assigns topics. Ninety-three percent said they use *only* online sources for a variety of reasons, mostly convenience. One student explained, "I tend to use Internet sources because they are the easiest to pull information from, and more importantly, it takes less time to find information online, which helps to keep from falling behind deadlines."

When deciding on which sources to use for research, 29 percent said that they choose the ones that seem the most "credible." It is unclear what meets their criteria for credibility, although one student wrote, "I check to see if it's credible by looking to see if it has all the things needed to make a proper MLA citation." This statement causes me concern, which I will elaborate on in later chapters.

One hundred percent of participating students said that they are given one week to start and finish a research project. Most students (86 percent) reported that they spend little (five minutes) to no time reflecting on their research process. Thirty-six percent admitted to using a citation service, specifically EasyBib, to document their sources, even when instructed to create citations from scratch.

Perhaps the most damning of the responses came from one student who wrote this in the "Additional Comments" section: "I often feel like we, as students, are not very encouraged to learn about and be interested in our topics, and are rather motivated by grades to learn how to recite facts in a new way instead of gaining a new understanding through our research."

We can do better than this.

Part of the reason students dread research is that we emphasize and demand perfectly formatted products, picky page lengths, the "right" sources and content (Ballenger 2015). These are the things we are showing students to be important when really it is discovery and learning how to learn that are the most valuable parts of research. We place value on formats, page lengths, content, and sources because they can be assessed easily.

Lately I've been wondering who grading is for exactly. More and more I'm convinced that grades are for teachers. Our work—what we actually produce—cannot be measured, so we seize on students' work to mark our own success. It seems the only thing we are truly measuring is compliance. Rubrics protect teachers; they don't assess learning. Yet we are bound to use them.

Research can be a tremendous learning experience provided that it is done as an investigation and not as fact grabbing. Some of the most precious aspects of research are setbacks, curiosity, and revisiting questions and information for new understanding and discovery.

How do we put a measure on setbacks or curiosity?

Many of us have difficulty with the idea of letting students pursue their own interests with research. There are plenty of reasons:

- We want to see only our content.
- We lack understanding of research, its process, and its benefits.
- Embracing inquiry in the classroom is out of our comfort zone.

- We lack knowledge of available resources and how to use them.
- We don't have enough time.

So, we are conflicted about the whole research thing, which, on a human level, is OK. What's not OK is depriving students of positive experiences in developing research skills. We aren't getting rid of grades anytime soon, but we can alter our attitudes toward research and its value in students' education. Here are two ideas:

1. Research is not a scavenger hunt. It's more like an archaeological dig on a construction site. You're making something, not checking off things on a list.

2. If we want to see whether students have memorized our content, give them a test. If we want students to internalize and transform our content, let them research.

In the chapters that follow I will suggest that we take a serious look at how students' experiences with research on the secondary level can be improved. I will encourage teachers and schools to consider the following:

- Embracing inquiry, curiosity, and exploration
- Teaching students to question
- Emphasizing the importance of reading in the content areas
- Recognizing and legitimizing what students are doing with research on their own
- Developing authentic projects that include immediate components of research (i.e., surveys, experiments, and interviews) and reviewing literature in content areas
- (Re)establishing the school librarian as an educational partner for teachers and students
- Assessing skills, not ideas

I acknowledge that much of what I mention and question in this book will be challenging to read and think about, let alone implement. Any growth requires some stretching. We need to start making research the learning tool it should be.

# Chapter 1

## A Question of Content: Topic vs. Inquiry-Based Projects

*I paint objects as I think them, not as I see them.*

—Pablo Picasso

Long ago, before I was an educator, my oldest daughter, Sarah, then a fourth grader, came home one day with a yellow sticky note carefully preserved between her thumb and forefinger. On it was written "Ruby Bridges."

"What's this?" I asked.

"My assignment," she said.

"What about Ruby Bridges?"

Sarah rolled her eyes. "Mom, I have to do a project on her."

That was all. There were no other instructions or encouragements. This scene took place long before digital resources were so prevalent, but even if my daughter had gone to a print encyclopedia and looked up "Bridges, Ruby," what would she have learned?

It turned out that Ms. Bridges had visited Sarah's elementary school as part of an enrichment program. She told her story and gave students signed copies of her picture biography. The students were allowed to ask her any questions they wanted. One brave boy asked if he could touch her hair. She let him.

So much has changed in the world of information access since Sarah was in fourth grade. What has not substantially changed is the way "research" assignments are framed. I put the word *research* in quotes because we misuse this word when we use it to describe the assignment Sarah received. The assignment she received was to write a report. There are times and places when a report is appropriate and necessary, but it seems to me, in this situation, that research would have been a much more meaningful and less flat experience for students, especially after meeting and speaking with Ms. Bridges. Even as fourth graders, these students could have been encouraged to connect to what they already knew about civil rights to arrive at their own questions. Let's look at a classroom lesson that employs this strategy.

## Making an Invisible Process Visible

For more than a decade, I have spoken to classes of students about the research process, with limited success. In doing my own research, two things became apparent. First, most people these days perceive the research process as a straight line—and for good reason. We start with a one-word topic or name (Ruby Bridges), we put that word into a search engine, and we receive some information from which we generate a paper or a Prezi presentation.

Second, people have a very hard time coming up with a meaty question from which to begin their research. Extrapolating from Bruce Ballenger (2015) in *The Curious Researcher: A Guide to Writing Research Papers*, adapting the idea to secondary school, and drawing from my own observations, I have come to realize that very often people run with the "what" question and stop there. A person's first inclination is to define—for example, "What about Ruby Bridges?" This question leads a person to encyclopedic sources where he will no doubt find birth dates, lists of significant accomplishments, and so on. If facts are all that is required, this assignment can be completed, start to finish, in an hour. It's entirely possible that some students will complete it in the very hour before it's due.

Believe it.

I asked students and they told me so.

In front of witnesses.

If we want our students to transform information, then we must get them to a place where there is a much heftier question that leads to higher-order and critical thinking about information. So, how do we do it? Let's peek at my lesson.

My lesson has two objectives:

1.  Making the research process visible to students

2.  Busting them out of the definition—or "what"—mode so we can get to a better question

To begin the lesson, I draw a diagram on the board of the "What" Model (Figure 1.1), which I've just described. It looks like this:

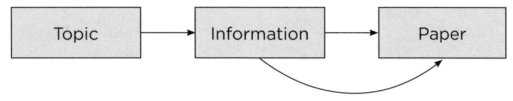

**Figure 1.1** The "What" Model

Notice that this model doesn't resemble the investigation scenario I posed in the introduction. I start by showing students a list of possible topics. They acknowledge that they are familiar with choosing a topic from a list.

"So, you get your topic and then what?"

"Go to Google and type it in."

"What happens next?"

"Information."

"Then what?"

"Write the paper."

At this point, I show them the "What" Model, pointing out that it's a straight line. They agree that this is an accurate picture of how their research assignments go.

Next, I mention that there's a piece missing. I tell the class that I'm about to draw a picture of the research process mixed with a baking metaphor (Figure 1.2). I draw a big bowl on the board. In the bowl I write, "Your knowledge, Your understandings, Your assumptions, Your questions, Your experiences." I explain that the bowl represents each of them individually. Everyone starts with some ingredients in his or her bowl. These ingredients come from their reading, learning, interactions, news, family values, and so on—everything they've taken in over the course of their lifetimes.

Brazenly mixing metaphors, I also suggest that they could think of their knowledge as an unfinished jigsaw puzzle that they will work on for the rest of their lives. Pieces that fit become their knowledge forever. Sometimes we get pieces that don't fit right away but may fit later, after we've filled in more pieces. Everything we learn connects to something we already know, and that's where the pieces fit. The bowl of ingredients represents what they already know.

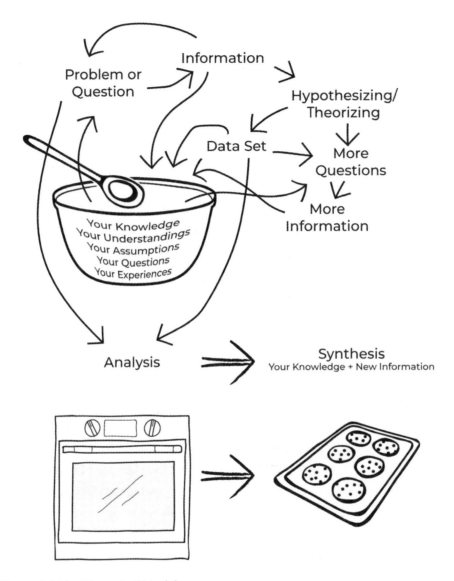

**Figure 1.2** The "Recursive" Model

As I'm drawing, I model the connecting knowledge idea by referencing previous assignments they have done. We need to impress upon students that what they already know is integral to fruitful research. This is the time for them to use all that content they've been collecting.

During one lesson with sophomores, I referred to a project I knew they all did in freshman English. To increase background knowledge before reading *To Kill a*

*Mockingbird*, students were given a choice of photos to work with from either the Great Depression or the civil rights movement. They researched the events that led to the snapping of the photo and then created a piece of historical fiction writing that featured a character from the photo or someone made up entirely. I tell them (to their surprise) that in doing that project they created new knowledge. I continue to draw the diagram that shows how the information flows during the research process. I point out the circular motion of the information flow and contrast it with the flat and assembly-line-like "What" Model.

For research to be real, there must be discovery and a transformation of the information into something new—hence, creating knowledge; this is represented in my drawing as a plate of warm cookies. No two people's cookies will taste or look the same, because the ingredients they start with and then add will invariably be different. I explain that *synthesis* is putting two typically unrelated things together to form something new, and that the two things in this case are their prior knowledge and the new information they find. I note the presence of the oven, and that there needs to be a time of analyzing and thinking that helps to finish the creation.

Finally, I point out that this process cannot be completed the night or hour before the project is due. (Even "mad geniuses" need time to allow ideas to coalesce in their minds.) I mention that most researchers are left with unanswered questions at the end and that this is perfectly normal. More questions lead to further study, and that benefits all of mankind.

Although this metaphor may seem lighthearted, it is based in some very sound research. In fact, this lesson demonstrates the transactional theory of reading developed by Louise Rosenblatt:

> The reader approaches the text with a certain purpose, certain expectations or hypotheses that guide his choices from the residue of past experience. Meaning emerges as the reader carries on a give-and-take with the signs on the page. As the text unrolls before the reader's eyes, the meaning made of the early words influences what comes to mind and is selected for the succeeding signs. But if these do not fit in with the meaning developed thus far, the reader may revise it to assimilate the new words or may start all over again with different expectations. For the experienced reader, much of this may go on subconsciously, but the two-way, reciprocal relation explains why meaning is not "in" the text or "in" the reader. Both reader and text are essential to the transactional process of making meaning. (1995, 26–27)

Students should be cognizant of their own learning process and understand that what they already know is considerable and very, very important—it is how they make meaning of new information. They need to trust themselves as learners, and we must show them that they are more than vessels into which we pour our content. This segue leads me to the second part of this lesson: getting to a hefty question.

For this particular project, the teacher had given his students a four-page list of potential topics (see Appendix A). I picked Jackie Robinson from this list and wrote his name on the board. I asked students what they knew about Mr. Robinson. Here's what we generated:

## Jackie Robinson

Baseball

African American

Played for the Dodgers

Broke color barrier in Major League Baseball

At this point I asked students by show of hands whether they thought they could write a paper on Jackie Robinson with only the information we had just shared. (On one day, I did this lesson in six classes of juniors—ranging from honors to general level—and in each class about half of the students raised their hands.) I followed up with, "How many of you have actually written a paper this way in the recent past?" Again, about half of each class raised their hands. "Successfully?" (We established that "success" in this case would be to turn in the aforementioned paper and receive a grade of 83 or better on it.) Once more, half of the students raised their hands. Their teachers were present as I conducted this lesson. I was amazed by how honest the students were about their work ethic.

"What do you do next?"

"Go to Google and type in *Jackie Robinson*."

"What will you find?"

"Stuff about Jackie Robinson."

After this discussion, I pulled out an encyclopedia article about Jackie Robinson and showed it to them. I told them that I did just what they usually do, but I didn't use Google. Instead I went to one of the library databases and typed in *Jackie Robinson*. I found a wonderful biographical article about Jackie Robinson and did what they usually do: read the first paragraph. I read aloud that paragraph, which included the information we had already listed on the board but with a couple more details. I explained that this process had thus far led me to facts, because "what" questions are questions of definition. I added that most of the time people stop there and begin writing, but this time we would go beyond the "what." I asked them what the most interesting fact on the board was, and they answered "Broke the color barrier." So, I mentioned that, from reading the first paragraph, we learned that Jackie Robinson achieved this feat in 1947. I asked them to think about the civil rights research they had done the previous year.

"When was *Brown vs. the Board of Education*?"

"1954."

"When did the major civil rights movement take place?"

"1960s."

"Right. Ruby Bridges singlehandedly integrated a school in New Orleans in 1960, thirteen years after Jackie Robinson did it in Major League Baseball. Why was Mr. Robinson able to accomplish desegregation of baseball so much earlier than the desegregation of schools in the United States?"

There is no ready answer to this question. It has to be conjecture. A guess. This is unfamiliar and uncomfortable territory for students. I was prepared for silence when I asked, but excited because now they were actively thinking and approaching a meaty question that could lead to a claim/thesis/hypothesis. I pointed out two important things I had just modeled in case students missed it. First, I asked a question other than "what." I asked "when," which led to other questions. Second, I accessed their prior knowledge about civil rights.

Next I asked, "Why do we watch baseball?"

"America's pastime!" "Entertainment!" (I'm leading students here purposely for the lesson. When I work with them one-on-one, I encourage them to play around with their own questions and observations. Time constraints play a role in how relaxed students feel through this process. Panic can set in. We work through it.)

"Do you think people had an easier time accepting desegregation when it came to entertainment? Let's say this is the case. We can turn this question into the claim *People don't care about your color or race if you're entertaining them.*"

Now we are set up for a compare/contrast engagement with information. Students can compile a data set by looking at the experiences of workers, athletes, students, entertainers, and so on during the period of desegregation in the United States. Who were others that broke color barriers in their respective fields? Who had it harder? Was it "easy" for any of them? They can draw examples from current popular culture, like the *Hidden Figures* movie. Why were there differences in the treatment of certain people?

After all of this discussion, one student said, "But this is supposed to be a paper on Jackie Robinson."

"Well, I'm sure he will be featured heavily in the discussion within the paper, but isn't the direction we took it in much more interesting than a simple report on Jackie Robinson's life?"

They all agreed it was.

## Making Something Out of Their Education

Research writing—the process itself—is a creative pursuit. Yes, there is an academic bent to the product of research, the paper or presentation of it, but the act of conducting research is inherently a personal one. Bruce Ballenger says, "[S]tudents' own subjectivities are not only relevant to academic work but are also an inescapable part of it" (2015, xxii). He goes on to say that students don't see research as a "creative enterprise," and he wonders about the possible reasons:

> The answer in part, lies with the research paper assignment itself. It seems to encourage a very closed process of inquiry: Come up with a thesis quickly, hunt down evidence to support it, and wrap it up—all the while focusing less on learning something than on getting it right: the right number of pages, the right citations, the right margins. This isn't the way academics approach research at all, I've thought. We do research because we believe there is something to discover that we don't already know. (2015, xxii)

In picking up on Ballenger's point, the "assignment itself" can set students on the road to low-level thinking. I said before that there are times and places when a report is perfectly appropriate and the best measure of a student's level of memory of content. However, we must stop calling these types of assignments "research." There is no difference between copying facts on Thomas Jefferson from a website and looking up what time a movie is playing. In both cases, nothing is done with the information other than transmitting it, and the student will not retain much of it. These are the papers that end up in the recycle bin at the end of the year.

So how did we get here? The argument could be made, pretty convincingly, that we are seeing the effects of long-term, high-stakes testing and how it has adversely affected curriculum and instruction. Kelly Gallagher says that "when the No Child Left Behind (NCLB) legislation went into effect, teachers and administrators overreacted," resulting in a pivot toward "shallow exams" as well as other "assessments that valued lower-level thinking" (2015, 1).

In their research, Nichols and Berliner found that "high-stakes testing has harmed teaching and learning" and that these "tests undermine teacher-student relationships" and "lead to a narrowing of the curriculum" (2008, 14). Further, they observe that "Under pressure to prepare students to perform well in math and reading, teachers engage in repetitious instruction that boils down content to isolated bits of information, leaving little time to engage in creative interdisciplinary activities or project-based inquiry" (2008, 15).

Even worse, many assert that, under NCLB, the responsibility for learning shifted from students to teachers. Perhaps it was the punitive penalties bestowed upon schools and individuals for failing to make Adequate Yearly Progress (AYP) that caused this shift. It is definitely perceptible, especially to educators from other countries. "The U.S. is one of the few countries in the world that places virtually all the burden for learning on the shoulders of teachers. This notion is alien to teachers in most countries that are our competitors in the new global economy" (Gardner 2010). Miller and Lassmann share the same view: "[M]any have taken the position that NCLB intended for teachers to be the ones solely responsible for student learning. If the student fails, it is the fault of the teacher" (2013, 167). They go back even further, citing the National School Lunch Program, signed into law by Harry S. Truman in 1946, as the beginning of schools taking on the responsibilities of parents.

Whatever the reason, we as teachers must regain our focus on what is important. I stand with Kelly Gallagher, who says, "Remember that good teaching is not about 'covering' a new list of standards; good teaching is grounded in practices proven to sharpen our students' literacy skills" (2015, 7).

How, then, do we craft an assignment that will lead students to higher-order thinking? The answer lies in what we expect students to get out of doing the work. We must strive to move students toward the bigger questions and to connect new information to what they already know. The questions have to come from them, but we will need to model forming questions (more on this in Chapter 2). Instead of the directive to pick a topic and find facts about it, ask students to read widely on a subject and form a claim or set up a comparison with other things related to it. What surprises them? Which tidbit leads them to question(s)? What do they already know?

The bottom line here is that research is a process that takes time. If we are invested in the value of research, we must allow students more than a week to work on a research project. Ideally research should take place as a culminating activity after months of study of a particular subject. It is the ultimate authentic assessment. In his foreword to Umberto Eco's book *How to Write a Thesis*, Francesco Erspamer says this: "Umberto Eco takes us back to the original purpose of theses and dissertations as defining events that *conclude* [emphasis mine] a program of study. They are not a test or exam, nor should they be. They are not meant to prove that the student did his or her homework. Rather, they prove that students can *make* something out of their education" (2015, x).

## Assigning Topics vs. Allowing Students to Choose

Earlier I mentioned that, when left to themselves, students have a very difficult time deciding on a direction or question for their research. Experience has shown that it's more expedient for teachers to assign topics to students.

Assigning topics is a good thing for us to do. Donald Graves says, "About twenty percent of a writer's diet ought to be assigned" (1984, 192). After all, if one goal of education is to teach people to solve problems, then teachers posing some of those problems emulates real life—we don't always get to choose our troubles or pick the ones that are easiest to handle. (More on real-world applications in Chapter 7.) My concern is that the research process gets lost when we simply give students a name to start with, as in the "Ruby Bridges" example.

There is a caveat to assigning topics to students. Graves goes on to say this:

> [A]n assigned topic requires preparation; it requires the writer to read, interview, find the voice of opinion and concern in wrestling with the facts. Assigned topics mean that the teacher participates in the process of gathering data. Students see the teacher go through the process of doing the assignment with them. Modeling is never more important than in assigned writing, particularly writing in the content areas. Modeling means that the teacher demonstrates topic discovery, brainstorming, reading and note-taking, drafting, and final copy. (1984, 192)

Modeling assignments for students does two things. First, it allows students to see the process worked out in real time: the grappling with finding the right research question;

the decisions about where to get the information; the reading, analysis, and proper use of that information; and, finally, the synthesis—a written piece created. Second, it allows us to see the inherent flaws in our own assignments. If we have trouble completing the work we assign, then surely students will as well.

We need to see that students can do something with our content besides mimic it, and that's another benefit of modeling. We would not choose a name from a list, look up facts, copy them, and hand that in as finished work.

## Then There Were Digital Resources

Part of the problem with student research lies in the ways technology has changed how we access information in the twenty-first century. We must adapt our instruction so that research in the digital age has meaning, shows evidence of real learning, becomes an authentic assessment of knowledge, and allows students to "make something out of their education." It is simply too easy to find facts; they are right at our fingertips at all times, and, let's face it, merely looking up stuff requires no thinking.

Kristen Purcell et al. (2012) conducted a study published by the Pew Research Center titled *How Teens Do Research in the Digital World.* Data were collected through an online survey of more than 2,000 middle and high school teachers who taught advanced placement courses or were part of the National Writing Project. They also conducted focus groups, which included some students, both online and offline.

Nearly 100 percent of the teachers surveyed believe that "the Internet enables students to access a wider range of resources than would otherwise be available" (2012, 2). It is absolutely true that we live in a time when we have many options for locating information. It is also true that students aren't being taught how to use the tools properly. The Pew study backs up this assertion. "Indeed, in our focus groups, many teachers suggest that despite being raised in the 'digital age,' today's students are surprisingly lacking in their online search skills" (2012, 5).

As with any other literacy skills (i.e., reading and writing), we operate under the assumption that high-school-aged students are at least proficient—a reasonable assumption in general. However, even among the highest-achieving students there are deficiencies in reading and writing, which real research projects throw into stark relief. Research demands close reading of informational texts, annotating, questioning, and the interplay of students' ideas and values with those of the authors. Our students lack the stamina to dig and sift through information.

Teens are programmed to find "answers."

Immediately.

With labels or headings that exactly match their topic words. (If websites or articles could say, "Talulah, the answer to your question is . . . ," that would be even better.)

Books are perceived as work; students prefer the speed of access online. The trouble is that online searches are not all that speedy when we consider the distractions and misguided hits that result from imprecise search strategies. With more and more computers arriving at schools daily, we have to get a grip on teaching and reinforcing information literacy skills across the board.

Even more troubling is the fact that the very definition of *research* has been altered by the Internet. The speed at which information can be located spurs the notion that research is something that can be done quickly. The Pew study addresses this concern as well: "[S]ome teachers report that for their students 'doing research' has shifted from a relatively slow process of intellectual curiosity and discovery to a fast-paced, short-term exercise aimed at locating just enough information to complete an assignment" (Purcell et al. 2012, 2). This finding is consequential. Real research leads to new knowledge, and learning requires time.

Research—the intense pursuit of answers—should occupy one's waking hours. It should pop up in one's thoughts at odd times of the night. It should prickle the intellect as a persistent itch prickles the skin. It should be a passion, a temporary obsession, page count unlimited. It should not be a pesky, tedious assignment. (*How many pages should this paper be?*) Most students at the secondary level are using the term *research* to describe fact grabbing. Unfortunately, we are the ones who gave them the term. The word *report* has negative connotations now, so we avoid using it, but there needs to be a clear distinction between the two forms in students' minds.

We must model the behavior of taking notes from sources gathered, putting them next to a weighty research question, and determining whether the information is relevant, contradictory, or earth shattering instead of sitting by while students open a Word document, leave a couple of Internet tabs open, harvest quotes from web pages, and then copy and paste them into the document, the resulting paper comprising information cobbled together from "sources" and showing no insight from the student. This process looks just like the "What" Model in Figure 1.1. The problem is perpetuated by topic-based "research" assignments. All these years later, we are still handing students yellow sticky notes with "Ruby Bridges" printed neatly on them and no other instruction.

## The Importance of Relevance

We are fortunate in our high school: our administration values collegial work. With their encouragement, I am part of several peer groups who are allowed time to come together for discussion and to work on improving practices over and above department meetings. One such group is our Writing Committee, which is composed of teachers in the core disciplines. This committee originally was facilitated by Linda Rief, who came in once a month to guide us through two-and-a-half-hour workshop-style meetings. Although the players have changed, the work continues, and it is glorious to have this time to revel in our own writing lives. This book is the direct product of my experience with the Writing Committee.

One day we were talking about how science teachers might see evidence of learning from students' writing. Every year the biology classes cover a unit on cancer, and students are allowed to choose a type of cancer to study. (Although choice personalizes the work for students, it strikes me as sad that there are so many cancers to choose from.) One of the teachers mentioned that the papers she receives from this assignment read like reports and reflect little or no discovery or connections. To combat this undesirable result, she and her faculty partners tried adding other aspects to the study, such as environmental factors, cosmetics, food, and so forth. Even with these added facets, the papers were not what she hoped.

If I were a student in biology class and we were going to learn about cancer, I would want to explore some of my own questions about the disease. I have been visited by cancer in the generations before and after me. My parents both died of cancer—lung and brain—and my daughter survived acute lymphocytic leukemia. I have lots of questions about cancer:

How and why is it that my daughter survived but my parents did not?

Does it have to do with lifestyle choices?

Does it have to do with age at onset of the disease?

Does it have to do with the type of cancer, or what organs it attacks?

Are older people with cancer treated differently from young people?

These questions are personal and mean something to me. I have often wondered how things would be for me if my parents had survived. I genuinely want to know the answers. If I were to pursue a study of cancer starting with these questions, I would have to compile a data set so I could examine information and statistics on cancer and age groups, environmental and lifestyle factors, the mechanics of each kind of cancer, the various treatment protocols of these cancers, and much more. I would really learn something.

With this idea in mind I suggested to my colleague that there is probably not one student in any of her classes who has not been touched by cancer. She agreed, as did all the members of our committee. Connecting to what students already know is where we should begin research projects with our students. We need to ask ourselves what we are looking for from students' research. (More on this in Chapter 6.)

Let's say that a social studies teacher is teaching a unit on the American Revolution. A topic-based project could be assigned by giving students a list of, for example, the Founding Fathers. Students would choose one of the names and set about "researching." The teacher is hoping that the student who chooses Thomas Jefferson includes the fact that Jefferson wrote the Declaration of Independence in his paper. Most likely the teacher won't be disappointed. However, the student should already know this fact from his fourth-grade class notes, so what was the purpose of the paper? The student poses no questions of his own about Jefferson's role in the Revolution. He doesn't discover anything new from the exercise. If this teacher wants to measure whether his content sticks with students, many other great assessments serve that purpose.

I see research projects as a chance for us to turn learning over to students. One of the most important things high school students should receive is the knowledge of who they are as learners. The real research project is an opportunity for them to discover not only the information on a particular subject but also how they went about learning from doing the research itself.

Research begins with inquiry. We must allow students to grapple with their big questions. The research process makes it possible for students to pursue an inquiry that is relevant—not just interesting—to them. Kylene Beers and Robert Probst express this notion very eloquently in their book *Reading Nonfiction: Notice & Note Stances, Signposts, and Strategies*:

> *Interest* is about something out there, out in the world. The video is interesting. The photographs are interesting. Interest is often fleeting, lasting about as long as the video clip we provided for kids to watch. *Relevance*, by contrast, is

always personal. Relevance is about what matters to you. It starts by observing something in the world, but it shifts to a thought or a feeling inside of *you*. Something that is relevant is inherently interesting; but something that is interesting isn't always relevant. (2016, 45)

Giving students latitude in their selection of research subjects would help the experience become relevant to them. If the subject is relevant, then the whole process of research will be too. Do we ever explain to students why we are assigning research? Do they understand how the work will benefit them in the class, the world, and their future lives? A good portion of the time, we are disappointed with the products of assignments, or, worse, we never receive the work from a percentage of the class. No learning goes on if students won't even try to do the assignment. We shake our heads and commiserate with our colleagues; then we go and give the next batch of students the same assignment and expect a different result. (See "Assigning Topics vs. Allowing Students to Choose" on page 14.) We are setting kids up to plagiarize.

## Depth Is Kind of a Big Deal

As content-area teachers, we struggle to cover a tremendous amount of material each year. Because of the need for breadth of curriculum in the core disciplines, there isn't time to explore much of it in any depth. Here is another great purpose for the research assignment. Students can choose an area of study within the discipline that is relevant to them and study it in depth, following their inquiries. These assignments need not be extensive term papers; students can do high-quality research using the argument paper or solving a local problem as a vehicle.

We will need to be open-minded about the direction the study takes. What is relevant to us may not be relevant to our students. The idea here is to release the power of learning to the student, so she can "make something" out of her education. History may make more sense to a particular student if she can see it through a different discipline or lens, such as mathematics or science. We can weight assessment of the skills more than the ideas so that students are free to make connections that are unique to their own thinking (see Figure 1.3).

Let's go back to the American Revolution. The colonists were outmanned, outgunned, and, arguably, disorganized. How could they have even hoped to win this war? What tactical advantage did they have? Mathematically this conflict should have been a slam-

Ms. Berry

Freshmen sem

10/13/17

Hunting for the youth

Hunting isn't just about the the kill, it a great way to teach children the importance of patience or it can give them a place where they can bond with their family and connecting with nature too.

Patience is key in hunting because you sitting alone or with a friend or family member in the woods,motionless,silent for hour on end and not even see a squirrel. The patience you gain from hunting can be used in other places in life, like at school or even down the road when you have a job. It's all about gratification. It seems that we have been almost programed for instant gratification but with so practice we can delay the grartifcaon ("Patience is Power"). A hunt that lasts for five hours is more gratifying than a hunt that lasts five minutes.

When I'm out hunting with my dad or grandfather it gives me a time to talk to them without dissection of life or what's happening in the world around us. When I'm in the treestand with one of them I can talk to them about anything from how life is going to stupid stuff like what we'd do if there was a zombie apocalypse. Huntting has brought me and my family closer it turned a good relationship to a great one(Dealing with Your Parents).  This quality time with them makes it easier to talk to them about the more difficult topics.

**Figure 1.3** Example of work in which we see a student take a unique approach and view of hunting. This paper is brief, and I wanted more! (More student papers appear in Appendix C.)

Hunting can make you more intune with nature like how the Native Americans were when

they were here (Paytiano). When you're just sitting in a treestand you see more of the beauty of

nature than just trudging through the forest. So believe that the animals sacrifice themselves for us

to consume (Paytiano).

Hunting is far more than just a kill. It's about building relationships and growing as a

person. And seeing the true beauty in nature.

Paytiano, James. "A Deer Hunt." The Native American Experience, Primary Source Media,

1999. American Journey. Student Resources in Context,

link.galegroup.com/apps/doc/EJ2156000349/SUIC?u=nhais_hdpm&xid=10d71ba9.

Accessed 13 Oct. 2017.

Orloff, Judith, "Phsychology Today: The Power of Patience," Sussex Publishers LLC. Sep

18,2012.

https://www.psychologytoday.com/blog/emotional-freedom/201209/the-power-patience

**Figure 1.3** (continued)

dunk for the British. Why did the British ultimately lose? What factors came into play that they didn't expect, and why couldn't they adapt? What kinds of munitions or tactics would have been more effective against the colonists, and why?

Any one of these questions could lead to a deeper study of the American Revolution than class time would allow. Students could do research and then present their findings and understandings to the rest of the class. In a couple of class periods, every student's understanding of the American Revolution could be deepened exponentially by capitalizing on unique approaches to the study of the event. This type of assignment might make the idea of research more appealing to students, and it would make their presentations far more enjoyable.

# Chapter 2

## Where Do Questions Come From?

*It is our attitude at the beginning of a difficult task which, more than anything else, will affect its successful outcome.*

—William James

In the fall of 2016, we brought back Freshman Seminar to our school. We had run this course before, but it was discontinued for a couple of reasons. First, not all freshmen were scheduled to take it their first semester. However, the curriculum was introductory in nature and included the mission of the school, various services provided (guidance, administration, library, nurse, clubs, etc.), and more. By the time second semester rolled around, students no longer needed an introduction to the school. Second, it was a pass/fail class not required for receiving a diploma—a back-burner class. In short: nice idea, implementation needed improvement.

In the five intervening years since dropping Freshman Seminar, we hired an outstanding technology integrator, implemented a 1:1 environment at our school, and developed some great anti-bullying, making-good-life-choices units that needed a place to be delivered. This course presented an excellent opportunity to teach and reinforce skills such as research, literacy, and technology that cannot be taught in isolation. I had great hopes for contributing to the success of the course this time around.

All freshmen were scheduled to take the seminar their first semester. Two social studies teachers, a resource teacher, the technology integrator, and I designed a curriculum that included two projects in which students could learn and use research, technology, and literacy skills. The course naturally became academic and now has a grade attached to it.

The major project was built around a SMART (Specific, Measurable, Agreed-upon, Realistic, and Time-based) goal. Students identified an area in which they felt they needed improvement—some wanted better time management skills; some wanted to improve athletically, academically, or musically. They read about the area and learned what they needed to change in their lives to make the improvement. Our tech integrator showed them how to use various applications and digital tools to record and track progress. They interviewed a person they perceived as a "professional" in their chosen area of study to use as a primary source. It was a rigorous project that they were given five weeks to complete.

For my part in this SMART goal project, I slowed the research process down significantly. We gave students specific research tasks along with lessons on topics such as how to locate good information, evaluating the information for quality and relevance, rhetorical language and writing, note-taking, analysis, synthesis, and citing sources using Modern Language Association (MLA) format. Every student had a computer, but we deliberately had them take notes by hand at first and asked students to construct citations themselves rather than use EasyBib or other citation-generating applications. (More on citation generation in Chapter 5.) They had never done a project this way before, and a good number of them resisted, saying that they already knew how to do research. Although we prepared students beforehand, I expected this reaction. Copy-and-paste habits are hard to break. Moving beyond the "what" question (see Chapter 1) is scary and requires a bit of faith.

The assessment for this project was a reflective essay that included graphics, charts, and photos and incorporated what students learned from their reading and about themselves, along with the interview notes from the primary source. Figure 2.1 is an example of a student's final paper.

I provide this example in its entirety because it shows that the student learned something from his research. He wasn't exactly successful in meeting his goal, but he thoroughly analyzed the data he collected and now has a better understanding of what he needs to continue working on. That finding is significant. Every study I've ever read ends with more questions and identifies areas in need of further study.

Ms. Berry

Freshman Seminar

December 12, 2016

## Remaking a Dream

My goal at the beginning of this project was to run 6000 feet without stopping. The thought of me  going outside and being more active gave me this fire in me; this emotion of wanting to be an athlete again. A craving you can say. Ever since my injury, I couldn't run. I pretty much broke my neck a couple years ago. I was at my third National Competition in TaeKwonDo and was in a fighting match with this kid in my division. He landed a round-house kick to my temple, severely tearing my ligament in my neck. The kick was so powerful that I got knocked out and went straight to the infirmary. I don't remember much after that..

I was on bed rest for two years. Going in and out of doctor appointments more than a couple times a week. Having therapy lessons on how to walk again, how to do normal "human activities" again. I look back on how I could've done something differently, if I could've blocked the kick. Giving me regret and a disappointment towards myself. I could've went to Rio De Janerio, the Olympics this year. Though because of this one incident, my life changed forever. Burning everything I worked so hard for, everything I love. Now just a fixed ember in the back of my mind to never be reignited again.

Now, with this project, I feel like I have the opportunity to make a change. To try and forget about all the bad. Though, I'm still holding onto what I accomplished, but it saddens me still  that I

**Figure 2.1** A student's SMART goal paper

lost it all. My old life, my sport that I love. The adrenaline of competing. So this is more of a personal goal to me. To make myself who I want to be again: an athlete.

To make all of this to actually happen, I have to think about many things. I already know that I can run 3282 feat without stopping so I just need to compare that with my goal (6000ft). I also need to know how I can show that I actually completed my goal. Puting the motivation in me, finding it and keeping it with me also. I already have a purpose on why I'm doing this, as I explained in the last paragraph anyways. I need to figure out on where I'm going to run, where I'm gonna keep track of all the days I've been inching closer to the goal. A log anyways. I also had to think about the season where we are in now. It's winter and running in the cold and snow will be tough on your body really. Without all the proper ways to prepare and execute the running all together, I will say that you will have injuries. I needed to know this so that it wouldn't happen to me.

I needed to measure my goals somehow. Luckily I found these two apps called

"Nike+Run Club and Nike+ Training". On these two apps there are ways that you can track your running distance, your amount of time it took you to run the specified distance. It also keeps track of where you are and paints a map on where you ran. It's pretty cool and I'm glad that I found these two when I did, because I will tell you that these two apps made this project so much

**Figure 2.1** A student's SMART goal paper (continued)

easier. (Collecting data wise). All I had to do was focus on my running without having to worry about what the time is or how far I ran. The app would talk to you saying things like "Halfway there! Keep it up!" So basically it motivates you to keep going, which really helped me throughout this project.

After I ran, I would save my workout that day and store it onto my phone. Keeping all the data that I need on a couple pictures. After a week of running, I would then look back through those pictures and look at my data. I would then copy my data that I've collected and put it into a more organized place called a spreadsheet. The spreadsheet on google drive is helpful due to the ability on graphing your data and overall is a well kept space for your research. The spreadsheet is very organized too so that you won't have to worry about getting things all jumbled up.

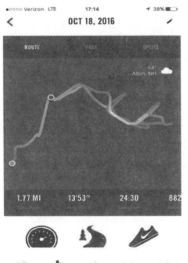

I categorized my data into different categories such as weekly distance goal, the distance I ran that day, the date, and if I made my weekly distance goal (Saying yes or no). I made a couple charts, one being the difference between the completion days and non-completion days. Another being the difference between the amount of distance I ran and and the date of that day.

My spreadsheet gave me a good look on how well I did throughout the project. It also showed me me the total data that I collected throughout this project. Not to mention showing me my active days and non-active. It gave me a comparison on how far I ran each day and if I reached my goal or not. One thing that I

**Figure 2.1** A student's SMART goal paper (continued)

noticed throughout my spreadsheet was my streaks of not running that day. I had gained shin splints throughout this goal and it was pulling me back. After I finished recording all of my data, my spreadsheet told me that I failed to complete my goal. I was 500ft off from my goal of 6000f and knowing this kinda disturbs me because if I had given that extra percentage on each run, then I might've ended up with different data. Overall, maybe my goal could've been complete. To look back though, I remember that I would always give my all from that last few hundred steps. Which raises the question to me that "Could I have done better"?

I was not successful on running 6000ft without stopping. I would say my major set back was shin splints blocking my days of training. That was a good streak of non-active days too so my stamina could've easily went down drastically. It's like being sick and when you're recovered your trying to recover from all that missed work done. Same with shin splints, your pain goes away, but your body isn't used to running everyday. I will tell you though that it kind of sucks. Like you really put your heart and mind into a goal and you've yet to finish it because something ridiculous comes out of nowhere and blocks you from your path. Something so ridiculous, like shin splints. It's a pain I will tell you that.

I have a few evidence of me actually doing my running. This particular one shows me training by running and stopping when needing to. Take note that I stop moving though at times. As seen on the picture, the outline that is a darker red or orange shows more intensity into the run. Unlike the more lighter colors like yellow and tan-orange, which shows my running pace slowing down more, sometimes even stopping in general. For this day I was actually at Prospect Mountain after school hours to watch my brothers Unified Soccer game. The thought came to mind that I could use part of that time to run so I basically did. There's a little data on the bottom of the picture showing my distance, average pace, and my distance.

**Figure 2.1** A student's SMART goal paper (continued)

This particular evidence that I've now shown you is me from the beginning of this project. I'm on Scott Drive, where my house is located. I just had done my daily run and decided to take a selfie. I've chosen this as my second piece of evidence due to it showing data and me actually participating in this goal and not just slacking off about it. The two important evidence in this is how long I ran and the distance it took me. That's the data I needed to log into my spreadsheet. This last piece of my evidence is apart of my nightly run if I was too busy during the daytime. I ohose this pieoe of evidenoe do to it showing and traoking my running throughout the time that I ran. I also like it due to that every tenth of a mile, the app speaks to you. It's a real motivation tool that really oame in handy. If I oould, I would've reoorded one of the ooaohes saying "keep it going, your doing good!" I didn't think about that until now.

**Figure 2.1** A student's SMART goal paper (continued)

The research that I did throughout this project gave me key tips on how to try and max the most out of my running. I learned important factors before I run, one being that I need to warm my body temperature up so that my muscles in my legs won't get inflamed. "If there inflamed then there's more of a possibility of injuring yourself even more, which can lead to some serious consequences" (Mackay, Jenny). *Men's Health and Fitness* also states that if you try and keep from striking down with your toes due to it bringing stress onto a calf muscles. Importantly I kept in mind on realizing when the pain started and stopped when it was too much.

I also had to make sure that I didn't just run. I had to put the time and effort into doing that extra stuff. For an example, I need to take in the consideration of doing the warm ups and not to mention the drills. According to my research; "Each drill will improve the aspect of good running and the form of it" (Coach Jenny HadField). I can say that I may have overdone with the running in the first part of the goal. My shins were starting to hurt and I knew that I was going to have shin splints. Even though I did not complete my goal, I still am proud on how well I did. How much I accomplished and mostly not giving up. Due to my pride, and the fire that was burning inside me, I just wanted to push myself so much. I just was so determined to run again and try become the person who I was before my injury. I can say that this project helped me realize how much I can really push myself. Even me getting shin splints didn't stop me from running, even though I could barely run. Shin splints just made me even want more. Wanting to work even harder, wanting to become somebody I once was again.

**Figure 2.1** A student's SMART goal paper (continued)

Works Cited

"9 Ways To Cure (And Prevent) Shin Splints - Men's Fitness." N.p., n.d. Web. 21 Oct. 2016

Brian.metzler. "Essential Form Drills For Speed And Efficiency | Page 2 of 10 | Competitor.com"

Compettiors. N.p., 2014. Web Oct. 2016

MacKay, Jenny. Track and Field. Detroit: Gale Cengage Learning. 2012. Print

"Winter Running Tips | ACTIVE." Coach Jenny HadField, h.d. Web. 24 Oct. 2016.

**Figure 2.1** A student's SMART goal paper (continued)

Research allows us to demonstrate advanced literacy. We read and learn new content, see how it fits with what we already know, and then we are ready to conceive of questions that require further and deeper study. As I mentioned in Chapter 1, most secondary school research falls short of the deeper parts of research: higher-order thinking, identifying problems, and questioning. Often our assignments as written compel students to stop at merely defining content, which makes research a passive activity that does not reflect what students have learned. They aren't allowed to draw on their own original ideas, which forces them into a familiar pattern of copying and pasting and (really) plagiarizing.

In a reflective piece, one Freshman Seminar student put it this way:

> Many authors publish information as if it is their own thoughts when in all reality we know that is not always true. If I type 9/11 into a search engine, millions of results will be thrown my way, 90% of it being the same regurgitated information time and time again, and that is similar to how school works. We often do research where we are asked to produce the perfect template of information that we could find a hundred times online. No sources are cited for all those unoriginal ideas, so I'm confused as to why I have to produce citations for the "new" essay I put out?

Our assignments stink. Students have noticed.

If we are being honest, this student's statement is very astute. She does not see the purpose for the research, understands that she's just moving information from one place to another, and is struck by the hypocrisy of our insistence on proper format and citations. She is not dealing with an important question or solving a real problem. It's boring work.

This problem isn't restricted to high school. "In an ideal academic world," says George T. Blakely of Indiana University East, "undergraduates would approach research paper assignments with excitement. They would regard them as fresh challenges and as opportunities to master and assimilate new material. But this is seldom the case. All too often, the assignment becomes a routine chore, which produces little more than mindless paraphrasing from reference works put together by bored students" (1997, 3).

## Student Attitude and Effort Toward Research

Following is a list of the behaviors I observe students exhibiting toward research:

- Overall dread of research projects
- Complaints that there's not enough time to do research
- Lack of investment—topics assigned by teachers; students almost never get to choose or develop their own questions to pursue
- Lack of stamina—students switch topics or thesis statements readily when the going gets tough
- Lack of ability to question
- Very little reading of, or willingness to read, information they find
- Avoidance of meaty or scholarly material
- Overreliance on Google
- Complaints about getting penalized for plagiarizing

We need to chuck these assignments.

I'm serious.

Why are we assigning this work? What good is it doing anyone? Why don't we use a project-based learning (PBL) model to create research assignments and make them responsive to disciplinary literacy at the same time? Using this approach, students will still get practice with and improve on their literacy skills, but they will be working with real, relevant, and timely questions that are interesting and allow them to make something real from their learning and our content.

When we assign a research project, we should consider the purpose for the work.

What outcomes are we looking for?

Do students need to show us that they've internalized content and can apply or transfer it to other situations?

Are we looking for signs of literacy?

Do we want to measure whether students can identify problems in our field of study (discipline) and offer possible solutions?

Do we want students to generate provocative questions?

In PBL, the learning goals are identified before the project starts—a sound practice. This approach would work well with research projects too. Why assign research projects? Most likely we will only see our own content coming back at us unless we identify and clarify learning goals. Have students consider the following: *What are the issues in the field? Who are the people discussing them? What do they have to say? Is there a local tie-in? Do the experts disagree? How does the content for the course fit in with the experts' discussions?*

Project-based learning (also known as problem- or product-based learning) is a perfect model for research projects. I am not suggesting that to have students do research we must adopt PBL. I am pointing out that the PBL model and the research process dovetail, and even overlap, in some places. For example, both begin with inquiry. In PBL this inquiry is most often student initiated—something I have been campaigning for in regular research papers. (I go into depth on helping students learn how to form good questions independently later in this chapter.)

Students identify and fill in their own knowledge gaps in PBL and in research. PBL is collaborative. Research can be collaborative. Teachers act as facilitators in both PBL and research. Students often develop their own assessments in PBL. In PBL students tackle real problems, and the projects are often displayed outside of the classroom. Student researchers on the secondary level and above should see themselves as creators of and contributors to the collective knowledge of mankind. (More on PBL in Chapter 7 and Appendix B.)

When I introduce the concept of disciplinary literacy to this discussion, things get exciting. Shanahan and Shanahan describe disciplinary literacy as "advanced literacy instruction embedded within content-area classes such as math, science, and social studies" (2008, 40). There's good news! We don't have to assign students a five-paragraph essay or give them lists of vocabulary to learn in order for them to improve their research skills. Yes, they will still have to read our content. Yes, they will have to write too, but we don't have to assign research papers in the traditional sense. And please, let's all accept that the five-paragraph essay does not exist in the world, aside from responses to standardized tests (Gallagher 2011, 232–233). It was created as a crutch for teachers and students who feel discomfort with writing and grading writing. It's time to leave this crutch behind.

I recommend reading David Labaree's essay "The Five-Paragraph Fetish" (2018), in which he demonstrates the (largely unintentional) damage that occurs when form is valued over meaning:

> The idea is to make writing easy by eliminating the messy part—making meaning—and focusing effort on reproducing a formal structure. As a result, the act of writing turns from moulding a lump of clay into a unique form to filling a set of jars that are already fired. Not only are the jars unyielding to the touch, but even their number and order are fixed. There are five of them, which, according to the recipe, need to be filled in precise order. Don't stir. Repeat.

Labaree shows how the five-paragraph essay pervades higher education, turning into the "five-section research paper" and then the "five-chapter dissertation" (2018). Why have students write if not to discover and make meaning from their reading and research? We must not forget the symbiotic relationship between decoding (reading) and encoding (writing). Labaree continues:

> Rules of thumb call for the writer to exercise judgment rather than follow format. Of course, it takes more time and effort to develop writerly judgment than it does to follow the shortcut of the five-paragraph essay. Form is harder than formalism. But the result is a text that does more than just look like a piece of writing; it makes meaning. (2018)

Sacrificing craft and creativity for convenience makes for functional and banal writing (just try reading the textbook) and the loss of an opportunity for discovery and learning. It's a shame that we hold such low expectations for student writing.

Tom Romano expands on these ideas in his book *Blending Genre, Altering Styles: Writing Multigenre Papers*. He says this:

> After junior high school—sometimes before—school is devoted to teaching students to think paradigmatically. The predominant mode of writing is exposition. There is little sanction in expository school for narrative knowing, unless it is written by someone published. Many teachers do not consider writing poetry or fiction cognitively rigorous. So the irony persists that while teachers might read plenty of imaginative literature—even revere it as some of the best word work people have produced—they funnel students' writing in its opposite direction. (2000, 22)

What if we approached student research in our disciplines the way it's done in the actual fields covered by those content areas?

For example, scientists in field ecology may study lichen, something most of us overlook on a regular basis. Why lichen? Here's where the definition, or "what," question comes in. Students read about lichen. How many varieties are there? Where does it grow? Is it unique to specific environments or regions? These are all questions that can be answered from the "what" part of this inquiry (the factual info out there to be copied and pasted). Once field ecologists know all these facts, what do they do? They might compare and contrast lichen with mushrooms or other vegetation that grows on tree bark. They might observe the growth patterns of lichen over time and record their findings and observations. They might apply various stimuli to lichen samples and record any changes. They will most certainly develop many more questions as they go on studying lichen. How does lichen react to certain pollutants? How does climate change affect lichen? How does lichen respond to rainwater versus tap water?

Students researching lichen as field ecologists do will be required to make many trips outside to study trees in the immediate area (or even beyond) over a defined period. This work is real. Students can be the first to discover new growth patterns, or species cohabitating as symbionts on trees. The report generated will not be a regurgitation of unoriginal ideas. It will be new knowledge that can be shared with the scientific community (and it will be much more interesting to read and write).

If we are not in an area with access to trees, we could have students study other life forms common to our immediate area. I used a science example here, but we can think of many different things that are studied by people in all sorts of professions that reflect our content areas. We might also consider the difference between qualitative and quantitative research studies. Certain fields lend themselves to qualitative study, such as social sciences, history, and literature, whereas in math and science fields the research conducted is most often quantitative.

The possibilities are endless. All that is needed is an open and inquiring mind.

Here are some ideas for each core discipline to get started:

| FIELD | RESEARCH TYPE | STUDY |
|---|---|---|
| History | Qualitative | -Look at leaders' styles<br>-Study the events leading up to war<br>-Read personal letters/diaries to compare eyewitness accounts with history textbook accounts (examining primary vs. secondary sources) |
| Literature | Qualitative | -Character study<br>-Author study<br>-Put literature/authors in the context of history<br>-Study societal concerns at time piece(s) were written |
| Science | Quantitative | -Conduct and report on experiments (physics and chemistry)<br>-Observe side (or unanticipated) effects (medicine/biology)<br>-Observe animals/life in the wild (biology) |
| Mathematics | Quantitative | -Proofs<br>-Apply math to solve problems in space; in physical areas<br>-Study number patterns and algorithms<br>-Theorize |

We can get students to think deeply and to form good questions about our content by creating a culture of inquiry in our classrooms. We need to be more receptive toward students' questions; we can use them to start discussions about our content, relate to students' interests, and connect to their prior knowledge. This approach takes us away from the traditional lecture style of delivering content and toward a more student-focused delivery. As with PBL, students are freer to contribute to and shape discussions, showing them that although they're not scholars in our content areas, their ideas have merit.

## Espousing a Culture of Inquiry

Recently I visited the doctor for a regular checkup and was compelled to wait for a time in the examination room alone. I looked around at the walls. There was a magazine display rack with a Plexiglas front. Scarlett Johansson peered at me from the front cover of *Marie Claire*. Three photograph prints hung on the adjoining wall. One featured a close-up shot of maple seeds. The next was filled with smooth, oval-shaped, colorful river stones. The third had a bedraggled leaf as its focal point. This grouping was obviously assembled to put visitors at ease.

What held my interest was not the prints or Scarlett Johansson—although she was quite fetching—but the rack that held, in tandem, two boxes of Halyard Sterling Nitrile Powder-Free Exam Gloves, Size Medium (Figure 2.2).

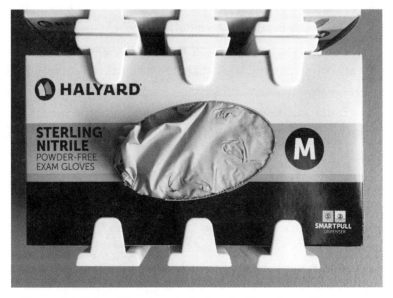

**Figure 2.2** Halyard Sterling Nitrile Powder-Free Exam Gloves, Size Medium

I wondered if *sterling* referred to quality or color—the gloves were a light gray. Then I pondered the various definitions of the word *sterling*. Next I wondered when, or how, I came to know the many meanings and uses of the word *sterling*. What had I done that revealed this information, and why did it stick with me? What curiosity led me to ask the question in the first place? Did I even ask a question? I remember my mother telling me that I'd received a *sterling* rose—they are exquisite and a unique color. I can remember someone described as possessing a *sterling* reputation, which I probably read somewhere. Why do I remember these things? The word has romantic connotations for me: is this why I own it in all its essences? It suddenly dawned on me that, in a short period of metacognition, I had generated multiple questions inspired by the most commonplace thing hanging on the walls of that examination room.

Students have a hard time coming up with research questions. I have stood before hundreds and delivered the joyful news that finally, *finally*, they could choose their own research topic—answer the question that has bothered them since birth—only to be met with blank stares, sometimes low groans, but mostly a stony and implacable silence.

What has happened to students' natural curiosity?

Any adult who has been trapped in a car with a three-to-five-year-old knows, with absolute certainty, that kids are *born* with questions. Have we teachers been so intent on delivering content that we don't allow inquiry detours in our classes? Do we think of the kids who do ask questions in class as "lesson derailers"? Are we modeling questioning in our classrooms? Do we honor the things students care about?

Somehow, during the process of getting students to comply with the rules of citizenship in the school community, we manage to squelch their natural curiosity. In so doing we consign ourselves to a career filled with reading boring, badly written, poorly cited reports. This trend can be reversed by opening the avenues to inquiry. In the book *Guided Inquiry Design*, Carol Kuhlthau, Leslie Maniotes, and Ann Caspari describe the first step in the guided inquiry process as "the open":

> The main challenge is to open students' minds and stimulate their curiosity. The open session inspires students to want to pursue the inquiry. The opener is designed to spark conversations about ideas and themes, pose questions and problems, and highlight concepts related to the subject. These conversations stimulate students to think about the overall content of the inquiry and connect with what they already know from their experience and personal knowledge. (2012, 51)

The key here is that teachers must guide students in the questioning of topics, ideas, and opinions. Inquiry in school classrooms is of the utmost importance. Americans enjoy advanced citizenship, which allows us to question our leaders. One of the biggest dangers to a society is a compliant citizenry; history is rife with examples of why that is a bad path for all concerned.

Questions that come from students directly have the best impact on their learning. Students receive much more from their education if they see how content connects to what they already know and value. In other words, any education/instruction/lesson is most effective if it is relevant. If students are given an opportunity to air, discuss, and follow their own inquiries, they are more likely to be engaged in the content, which is the goal for all of us. Students want to know all sorts of things that may affect them or that they're simply curious about. The freshman whose paper appears in Chapter 1 wanted to discuss what to do in the event of a "zombie apocalypse." Other, more serious questions might be *Why were athletes kneeling during the national anthem during football season? What's being done about the opioid crisis? How can we better treat people with mental illness? Does hair dye or tattoo ink cause cancer?* Cultivating an atmosphere of encouragement and safety in inquiry within our classrooms not only works toward the goal of engaging students in our content but helps with information literacy and research skills as well.

Real research leads to discovery. It begins with inquiry, but in order to form great research questions students must have a substantial amount of background knowledge—Ballenger calls it "working knowledge" (2015, 32)—from which to draw. The research questions students present can be very revealing.

Students have difficulty generating thesis statements. They tend to state facts that cannot be argued and therefore are not thesis statements. Students often stick with definitions, or the "what" questions, which invariably lead them to piles of facts. Facts alone will never lead to synthesis.

*Synthesis*—the act of putting together things that aren't usually connected to create something new—is the fruit, the critical higher-order thinking part of an inquiry. Without it, the student has merely regurgitated a few facts he could have stumbled upon in his own environment. The resulting product is not research. No real learning has occurred, and it is possible that the student already knew most of the information in the first place.

Students, wary of and uncomfortable with straying into the dangerous unknown, will stick to safe questions with ready answers. It is our job to press them to look at subjects from many different angles. We must model this behavior. Getting students to the point where they can develop a great argument independently takes some work and a firm resolve, but it's definitely worthwhile.

Over the years, I have had the opportunity to work individually with students in an advanced research class. One student was with me for the whole school year for independent study. He wanted to study basketball, a sport with which he was intimately familiar. The student had played basketball from a young age and, as a senior, was a leader on the school team. He also possessed a wealth of knowledge on past and present players and had a particular affinity for Michael Jordan, whose tenure as a player with the Bulls ended three years after this student was born.

I went out and bought books on all the aspects of the sport I could find: sports psychology, coaching styles, the "Dream Team" of the 1992 Olympics, players' biographies and memoirs, the genetic factors affecting athleticism, and on and on. We found research studies on coaching philosophies, statistics sheets on specific players that he identified, and op-ed pieces by authoritative sports writers from online sources. He was awash in information.

We spent an entire quarter reading widely on basketball with the goal of developing a viable research question. I had him write three short reaction papers to get him to annotate and work thoroughly with the resources. We compared all the heavy hitters against the ultimate player, Michael Jordan. We pored over statistics. We considered the phenomenon of the Boston Celtics dynasty in the 1970s. I cajoled. I framed. I reframed. I suggested we consider creating a list of criteria for what constitutes greatness.

My student never developed a good research question himself because I did not let him struggle with it. At the end of the year he wrote a detailed paper that demonstrated his ability to draw from many sources, but there were none of his own ideas in the text. My failure here was in doing too much of the heavy lifting in terms of thinking.

Rosenwasser and Stephen sum up this situation nicely in *Writing Analytically with Readings*: "A good paper is essentially the answer to a good question, an explanation of some feature or features of your subject that need explaining. If you don't take the time to look for questions, you might end up writing a tidy but relatively pointless paper" (2008, 61).

In my effort to make research a positive experience, I forgot that part of learning is experiencing setbacks and the joy of discovery. I spent too much time working on different angles. I did not give the student the space he needed to find his own questions.

In the end, I can only guess what his questions might have been had I allowed him to create his own data set.

In my mind, I contrast this story with that of another student who wondered why our school stopped having assemblies to honor local veterans. He discovered the reason: the student with the connection to the veterans had graduated. The young man aspired to join the military, and he saw the assembly as a sign of respect and gratitude. He wanted to know how we could bring this assembly back to our school. He asked his teacher, who advised him to go to the administration. The principal asked him if there was enough student interest to warrant an assembly. He didn't know the answer to that question, so he asked me. I suggested he conduct a survey of students. In the process of following through on the survey idea, he spoke to a paraprofessional who told him about the purpose and efficacy of petitions. Based on that conversation, he determined that, in fact, a petition would be a more expedient and effective way to accomplish his goal, so he set about creating one. He wanted to collect signatures electronically but didn't know how to do so. He made an appointment with the technology integrator, who showed him how to create the document he needed. Had he continued his work, this student could have presented a well-received petition to the principal. Unfortunately, for reasons unknown, he never followed through. Perhaps he became discouraged by his peers' lack of interest in his ideas.

Still, though this student faced setbacks and was redirected several times, in the end he learned how to petition for change. Although the product of his research was not a paper, he performed all the steps of the research process. He gained the tangible knowledge that he was not alone in his thinking and that some others shared the same values. He also came away with an understanding of what it means to be a citizen in a democracy by pursuing his own inquiry within a hierarchical organization. This is what we want for all of our students.

## Evolution of the Research Question

Zeroing in on a viable question with which to begin research can be harrowing, and it may be one of the most difficult aspects of conducting research. Some questions are too broad. These are the ones students typically come up with first. Some questions are surface level and will produce a list of facts if left unaltered. Ballenger addresses the development of research questions this way:

> Usually our initial research questions are questions of fact or definition: What is known about this topic? What is it? But a strong research essay needs *to do* something with the facts. One way to think about what a question is trying to do is to place it in one of these additional categories: questions of policy (ex: What should be done?), interpretation (ex: What does it mean?), hypothesis (ex: Might this be true?), value (ex: Good or bad? Best or worst?), or relationship (ex: Causes and effects? Similarities and differences?). (2015, 154)

My advice is to have students put off developing research questions until they read more about the subject. If students have trouble forming questions, ask them if they can identify a problem to be solved to start. It makes sense that one must know a bit about a topic before one can ask a good question or see a problem. A student should experience something—even vicariously—before he can develop sufficient feelings or interest to invest his time in thinking more about a subject. Often there is a whole vocabulary set that is inaccessible to him until he learns it from his reading. A student cannot converse intelligently about a subject if he doesn't speak the language.

So where do we begin? We start with the initial topic or subject—for example, human cloning (Figure 2.3).

## Making Connections: The Missing Piece

Students think it's witchcraft. It seems to them that teachers effortlessly come up with questions. Questions about stuff. They don't know how we do it. Students also self-censor—perhaps this happens after several years of our unintentionally devaluing their inquiries in school. The piece that's missing in student research work is their prior knowledge. I alluded to this idea in Chapter 1 and earlier in this chapter.

We do not encourage students often enough to draw on what they already know, to make connections to prior reading they've done, to think of our science content in a historical context. We are focused on what we must cover in class.

We forget that by the time they reach high school, students have been students for years. Doing the math, that's

10-week quarters = 40 weeks per year

40 weeks × 35 hours each = 1,400 hours per year

1,400 hours × 10 years = 14,000 hours

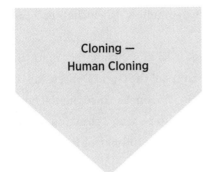

Cloning —
Human Cloning

- **Topic-in-a-Word — where most students start research.** The student may have little-to-no understanding of this subject.

Should humans
be cloned?

- **This is a yes/no question, but it is also a question of value.** The student is on the right track but the question is too broad. More reading needs to be done before the real digging begins.

Why has the government
stopped experiments/research
on human cloning?

- **Shows an early understanding of the problem to be solved.** A solution has been "found" — the government prohibits tests involving human cloning. The student is questioning why. Now we are getting somewhere! This question is the beginning of a good independent learning experience.

**Figure 2.3** Progression of a question

Our high school students have spent more than 10,000 hours in classrooms. They have absorbed a lot of content and other information. Plus there are the interests they pursue on their own time, such as theater, video gaming, music, and fishing. One student at our school surely has forgotten more about fishing than I will ever know—everything we discussed in Freshman Seminar he related to fishing somehow. (See Chapter 1 for more about modeling interdisciplinary connections.)

Students see their education as a series of boxes. In one is English, in another math, in a third science, and so on. It doesn't occur to students to connect the Great Depression to nutritional standards, or *To Kill a Mockingbird* to Jackie Robinson, because their school day is so regimented. When students are in history class, they aren't thinking about literature. They are listening to a lecture on robber barons, the Industrial Revolution, World War I, and so on. They take notes and focus on that content because there will be a test later, probably on Friday. Then, seemingly out of the blue, we ask them to come up with a great theory for a research paper.

When discussing the content of our disciplines in class, we are constantly making connections to things outside of that content ourselves, yet we do not often encourage our students to do the same. We can get very passionate about our subject. We have demonstrable feelings about it. We are bewildered that our students don't seem to care or share this passion. They check out, shut down. Students can't tap into our feelings because we aren't letting them. They remain passive and detached, sometimes to the point of not doing their work, and we blame it on their phones, laziness, their age. We don't know what to do about it, so we keep doing the same things over and over. Nothing changes.

In a previous section, I spoke of the language of our disciplines—the vocabulary. I also mentioned disciplinary literacy earlier in this chapter. I suspect a lot of us secretly believe that if English teachers brought back weekly vocabulary lists and put more time and effort into teaching them, our students wouldn't be so lacking in word knowledge. I challenge you to think about the vocabulary of your discipline. Do you devote time in class to teaching students the words they need to unlock meaning in your content? How can students be expected to form rich, thought-provoking questions if they aren't allowed to connect in their own unique way to our content—if they're not given the language to access comprehension of the subject? Vocabulary is a part of disciplinary literacy, along with approaching the reading, study, and content of our disciplines as a professional in the field would. We can use supplemental reading—articles and essays written by those in the field—to model how professionals work with new information and content. Sharing our own outside reading on the subject and what we learned from the piece(s) can help too.

People learn new vocabulary the same way babies and young children learn language. They listen to others speaking. They read. They listen to stories, meet others, go to stores. They see and hear words everywhere. Parents aren't giving their children word lists and testing them at the end of each week. Instead they point out new words and use them frequently in their speech. Kids are immersed in language, but their vocabulary is only as rich as their environment.

The vocabulary of research and academe permeates all disciplines. We not only need to make sure students are immersed in this language but also must point out that they've heard these words in other classes throughout their schooling and that professionals in our disciplines use them frequently. Here are some of the commonly used terms:

| | |
|---|---|
| critical thinking | problem solving |
| evaluate/evaluation | sources/resources |
| definitions/defining | plagiarism/plagiarize |
| copyright | assessment |
| analysis | synthesis |
| presentation | annotation |
| extrapolate | summary/summarize |
| bibliography | paraphrase |
| research | |

Of the seventeen words in the preceding list, fourteen are action words, and most of those are involved with creation. No coincidence.

Encouraging students to make connections needs to go further than pointing out common vocabulary. In class discussions, we can refer to other disciplines, cultures, popular art forms, and so on, and model how we make connections in our own minds. We can consult a curriculum map, which can be extremely helpful in highlighting for students the connections among disciplines. We can point out various themes that occur throughout history and examine how authors, musicians, and filmmakers have interpreted events. We can remind students of the science or math they've learned about in previous years and show them how those are used to help solve societal problems, such as a need for renewable energy or improving security on our beloved electronic devices. Probably the most important thing we can do to encourage students to make connections is to recognize when students are already doing it and provide them a safe environment in which to share their thinking.

I know. There is so much content and so little time. Yet if we make connections for students even briefly on a regular basis, they will see that it's a valuable exercise, and it may break down the dividers between disciplines. Everything is connected.

# Preliminary Reading on a Topic

Students should start reading authoritative essays expressing opposing viewpoints on their chosen topic. We can require an annotated bibliography and/or short (one-page) reaction papers in which students can highlight any new questions the reading brought up for them. (Figure 2.4 shows some examples of students connecting and reacting to their reading.) After reading and reacting may come relevance. If students have emotional responses to the reading, ask them to pinpoint what exactly caused them. That aspect of the topic is where they should be able to derive a good research question. This process takes some time, patience, and a lot of thinking. Rosenwasser and Stephen describe it this way: "Thinking and writing are recursive activities, which means that we move forward by looking backward, by repeatedly going over the same ground, looking for wrong turns, uncovering signposts passed earlier because of what we later discovered" (2008, 61). (This model is also discussed in the introduction and depicted in Figure 1.2.)

Where do we direct students to find these authoritative essays? If we've read any, we can share them with students. However, we probably won't have compiled articles on every topic students want to study, so the library is a great resource for books, digital resources, and periodicals (newspapers and magazines). Books and periodicals remain valuable resources for students, particularly for preliminary reading on a subject. Essays can also be found on various subscription databases such as Gale and EBSCO Host. The school librarian can tell students which databases are available at school or help them locate information in other places online.

Gale offers a database of essays from its popular print series Opposing Viewpoints. These essays feature authoritative pro-and-con viewpoints on a huge range of topics. Gale databases offer the added benefit of Lexile leveling, which indicates whether information will be accessible to students in terms of comprehension. There are other articles available on Gale as well, such as current journal or news items on various topics. These additional items appear on the same page as the pro-and-con essays; a student won't need to make multiple searches to view the additional material. In addition, a properly formatted MLA citation appears at the bottom of every article retrieved from Gale databases.

| **Monday February 19th** |
| --- |
| Source (citation): "Salem Health: Psychology & Mental Health." *Salem Health: Psychology & Mental Health*, by Nancy A. Piotrowski, One, Salem Press, 2010, pp. 114–119. |
| Significant Quote: "Two types of Alzheimer's disease have been identified: familial Alzheimer's disease (FAD), which follows an inheritance pattern, and sporadic Alzheimer's disease. Alzheimer's may exhibit early onset (younger than sixty-five years) or late onset (sixty-five years and older). Only 5 to 10 percent of Alzheimer's cases are early onset. Some forms of early onset Alzheimer's are inherited and often progress faster than late-onset Alzheimer's." |
| **100+ word quickwrite Research Journal entry - *consider addressing the following questions:*** <ul><li>What did you learn from reading this source today?</li><li>What is your reaction to your reading today?</li><li>What perspective does the author of this source present in regards to your research question(s)?</li><li>Why is this quote significant?</li><li>What does this quote mean in relation to your research question(s)?</li><li>What does this quote make you think about?</li><li>What further questions has reading this source raised for you?</li><li>What new potential search terms (phrases, names, terms, etc.) has this source given you?</li></ul> |
| One thing I learned from this quote is that there are two different types of Alzheimer's. Familial Alzheimer's disease (FAD), which follows an inheritance pattern and sporadic Alzheimer's disease, and this may occur in people younger than 65 years old or for people older than 65 years old. I was surprised to see that people that are younger than 65 years old that get Alzheimer's are inherited, progress faster than people who get Alzheimer's after 65 years old. And only 5 to 10 percent of Alzheimer's cases are people younger than 65 years old. So what I got out of this was that there are 2 different types of Alzheimer's. Some questions I have are: what triggers this to happen? Other than brain cell death. Some questions I have are: why people who got Alzheimer's when they were younger progress faster? What are the factors that go into that? Is it because they had the disease longer? Or is it something else? |

**Figure 2.4** Students connect and react to their reading.

**Tuesday February 20th**

Source (citation):
Turner, Susan M. *Homeless in America, How Could It Happen Here?* 2003rd ed., vol. 1, Thomson Gale, 2004.

Significant Quote:

"Virtually all Americans suffer illness and disease at some time in their lives, but for people experiencing homelessness and poverty, illness all too often means serious health concerns or premature death"

"Homeless people suffer from more types of illnesses, and with more harmful consequences than housed people"

**100+ word quickwrite Research Journal entry - _consider addressing the following questions:_**
- What did you learn from reading this source today?
- What is your reaction to your reading today?
- What perspective does the author of this source present in regards to your research question(s)?
- Why is this quote significant?
- What does this quote mean in relation to your research question(s)?
- What does this quote make you think about?
- What further questions has reading this source raised for you?
- What new potential search terms (phrases, names, terms, etc.) has this source given you?

Today I looked into an informational book that Mrs. Fraser recommended I look into. It is called Homeless in America, How Could It Happen Here? This book is packed with a lot of interesting/saddening information. It is a lot like some of the online sources I have looked into but a little less current. One thing that I chose to really focus on in this book was the chapter about the health of the homeless. One quote that really hit me was "Virtually all Americans suffer illness and disease at some time in their lives, but for people experiencing homelessness and poverty, illness all too often means serious health concerns or premature death"(Turner). I hadn't really thought of this all too much but homeless people don't have health insurance or in most cases don't have the ability or money to go to the doctor/hospital. This is extremely sad to think about because even something as small as the cold could get worse and worse and end up taking their lives. "Homeless people suffer from more types of illnesses, and with more harmful consequences than housed people"(Turner). This makes sense, but is very sad. Homeless people already have so much on their plates and health problems is just one more thing that adds onto this pile of struggles.

**Figure 2.4** Students connect and react to their reading. (continued)

| **Friday February 16th** |
|---|
| Source (citation): "Teen Health and Wellness." *Teen Health & Wellness*, www.teenhealthandwellness.com/article/119?search=suicide. |
| Significant Quote: Famous people who have struggled with depression include President Abraham Lincoln, journalist Mike Wallace, comedian Rodney Dangerfield, poet Sylvia Plath, statesman Winston Churchill, artist Georgia O'Keeffe, singers Janet Jackson and A. J. McLean, musicians Kurt Cobain and Gerard Way, and writers Virginia Woolf, Ernest Hemingway, and Mark Twain. |
| **100+ word quickwrite Research Journal entry - *consider addressing the following questions:*** <br> • What did you learn from reading this source today? <br> • What is your reaction to your reading today? <br> • What perspective does the author of this source present in regards to your research question(s)? <br> • Why is this quote significant? <br> • What does this quote mean in relation to your research question(s)? <br> • What does this quote make you think about? <br> • What further questions has reading this source raised for you? <br> • What new potential search terms (phrases, names, terms, etc.) has this source given you? |
| Depression is everywhere <br> in the air, in the soil <br> in your eye <br> everywhere. Everywhere everywhere. This is not something for the 'crazy people' as you can see. This is for the rich and famous, for the well-loved and popular as well. We do not need to be afraid to get help, in fact most depressed teens don't seek help because of the stigma associated with it. You could have a normal life, good grades, safe house, and still have depression. Mental health doesn't give a damn about your life, it comes to take over, convince you that you are nothing. |

**Figure 2.4** Students connect and react to their reading. (continued)

EBSCO Host is a portal to multiple excellent databases. Most colleges and universities offer EBSCO access through their libraries. Care must be taken in selecting databases on EBSCO Host, however, as some scholarly journals that are searchable through this portal may provide articles and research studies far too advanced to be useful to high school students. The school librarian can give students a tutorial on how to use EBSCO Host or other online resources to get the best results. EBSCO includes citation tools on their databases as well.

Consult your school librarian, who can direct students to all of the available resources. It is an excellent idea to have the librarian work as a partner for the duration of the project. If there are no librarians or databases at your school, look for the best essays and writing in your subject area. What and who are you and your colleagues reading to keep up with new research and developments in your discipline? We must read widely in our disciplines as well—that way we can give our students a great place to start their own reading. Information can also be accessed through your local town, college, or university library.

When a student begins to look for information for background reading, a general search will suffice. Once the student decides on a viable research question, search terms and parameters will have to get much more specific. I address this idea in greater detail in the next chapter.

# Chapter 3

## Have a Plan

*It is the responsibility of the student to explore his own world with his own language, to discover his own meaning. The teacher supports but does not direct this expedition to the student's own truth.*

—Don Murray

I am exceptionally lucky to live close to the University of New Hampshire, where many of the heavy hitters of literacy come to share their wisdom, experience, and ideas with others. Linda Rief, Penny Kittle, and Tom Newkirk are there nearly year-round. In the summer, a Literacy Institute takes place at UNH in which weeklong courses are offered to educators by real practitioners. Tom Romano teaches a course here every year. Educators come from all over the world to attend these professional development opportunities, and they're right in my backyard. Through these practitioners we also have vicarious access to two who have gone before us and whose influence is still felt keenly—Don Murray and Donald Graves. I was not fortunate enough to meet either of these gentlemen. Mr. Murray died in 2006, and Dr. Graves died in September 2010, while I was in the second semester of an MEd program at UNH. These two men were trailblazers in the field of writing instruction. To this day, their presence is felt; their work is constantly referenced by those who learned directly from them, and they are quoted often in professional development literature.

Recently I collected as many of Don Murray's books and essays as I could find, and I'm working my way through them. I am finding him a kindred spirit. What he discovered about the writing process over the course of his lifetime applies wholly to the research process. In fact, Murray spent most of his career promoting the idea that writing should be taught as a process, with emphasis on the learning and discovery rather than on a product. In his 1972 essay titled "Teach Writing as a Process, Not a Product," Murray says, "The student finds his own subject. It is not the job of the teacher to legislate the student's truth" (Newkirk and Miller 2009, 4). Donald Graves spent decades researching the writing process. He offers another sentiment in his essay "Balance the Basics: Let Them Write," in which he says, "When children are able to see their own writing used by others, their concepts of themselves as writers are heightened. When writing is not just a context between the child and the teachers but serves a broader audience, the teacher does not have to attend continually to correcting technical errors but can concentrate on other matters essential to good writing" (1984, 72).

In the spirit of Don Murray and Donald Graves, I submit that for research to become the valuable learning experience it should be, we must focus our efforts on teaching and celebrating the process rather than showing our students that we value only the product (and that the product had better reflect our content and be properly formatted). We must stop throwing the baby out with the bathwater.

There are no straight lines to the research process. I showed in Chapter 1 that it is a messy, circular endeavor that cannot fit neatly within the confines of a week's time, yet we must impose time limits and deadlines on our students. In this chapter, we are going to examine how allowing students planning time for research and locating and evaluating sources is key to successful, fruitful searches; then we will look at how to help students extract and organize pertinent information from the sources they choose.

## Benefits of Planning Research

Our school library is a busy, active place, especially since we acquired twenty-seven Chromebook laptops (in addition to the five desktop computers available for students to use). And, with the four-year phase-in of a 1:1 environment under way, there will be even more computers in the building in the coming years. We circulate tons of print fiction, which is outstanding. Students are reading, reading, reading. What alarms me is the trend I'm seeing in students' research practices.

In worrisome numbers, students come to the library to use the computers for "research" with no plan. They just dive right in to the paper-writing stage in the interest of getting it over with. If I suggest the use of print material—which may in fact be the best, most efficient resource for their purposes—they either look at me like I'm totally nuts or they politely take the book or periodical, set it on the table, and go right back to Google. They have already clicked into the groove of their established habits, and it will be a challenge to change them at this point.

In an ideal situation, all students embarking on research projects would come to the library equipped with a plan that would include an idea of the topic or subject of study, key search terms, and a list of places to look for the information they will use to begin background reading.

In Chapter 2, I said that students need to read widely on a subject before they can develop good questions. That takes time. Now I am suggesting that students form a plan before they begin research. That will take even more time. The benefits of investing the time frontloading before research are immeasurable. If students are shown how to determine their information needs, they will spend less time spinning their wheels while locating information, they will find high-quality sources that are relevant to their study, and they will be able to spend more time engaging in a meaningful way with the material, thereby discovering and learning more. A side-by-side comparison of the two research habits highlights the difference in approach to the task:

| STUDENTS' TYPICAL RESEARCH HABITS (CLOSED INQUIRY) | WHAT RESEARCH COULD BE (OPEN INQUIRY) |
|---|---|
| Student is given a one-word topic | Student is given a one-word topic |
| Student is brought to a computer lab and set loose | Student reads about the topic from multiple sources |
| Student plugs word into search engine and clicks | Student develops questions based on reading and connecting information to what he or she already knows |
| Student opens new Word document to begin writing paper | Looking at the nature of the question, the student decides what sources will yield the best information for his or her study and uses selected key search terms to locate information |

| STUDENTS' TYPICAL RESEARCH HABITS (CLOSED INQUIRY) | WHAT RESEARCH COULD BE (OPEN INQUIRY) |
|---|---|
| Student skims sites for information | Student accesses and selects sources, reads material, takes notes, checks relevance against research question(s), combines new information with prior knowledge, develops more new questions, and engages with material |
| Student copies and pastes facts into open Word document | After analyzing material, student draws conclusions and identifies his or her audience |
| Student cobbles together a paper using facts from sources (this action is plagiarism), formats paper and citations, then submits it to the teacher | Student synthesizes new information with prior knowledge |
| Student receives grade | Student creates presentation that shows his or her thinking and new knowledge |
| Student throws graded paper in the trash | Student shares new knowledge with his or her audience (stakeholders/ community), noting areas where there are still unanswered questions |
| | Student receives the satisfaction of learning and discovery, is motivated to learn more; a grade is given |
| | Community benefits from student's new knowledge; retains student's work |

Students tell me the process on the left side of the chart can be completed in the hour (or less) before the time the paper is due (see Chapter 1). The process on the right side of the chart takes much longer—probably a month. Look at the difference in value for the student (and everyone else)!

## Google Is Not a Place

Too often I have seen students who are conducting "research" stumble upon information in a haphazard way that involves lots of time scrolling and leaves them open to misdirection and distraction. When I ask them where they go to find information for their project (or anything else, really), invariably the answer is "Google."

Google is a corridor with many rooms and hallways going off it.

Google is a hub.

Google is a wormhole.

Google is a portal.

Google is *not* a place to go for information.

The word *Google* is so ingrained in our lexicon that it's no wonder students think of it as a place—maybe a large space station out there somewhere. Google has even become a verb:

**Goo-gle v.:** to go to a giant Internet portal, ask it a question, and receive millions of answers

**Goo-gled; Goo-g-ling**

*I Googled John Adams and received 627,538 hits.*

In his book *How to Find Out Anything,* Don MacLeod says, "Google is the Schrodinger's cat of search engines—it's simultaneously the greatest boon to online research ever invented and the archnemesis of effective information gathering" (2012, 30).

So how do we break the Google-as-a-destination mind-set? A couple of things should happen before students even go to the computer. Students should decide what type of search they need to embark on based on what they want to study. They need to determine their information requirements *before* they start searching.

What type of research will the student be doing? Action research requires generating a data set, as in the example in Chapter 2 where I described the Freshman Seminar SMART goal project. A review of literature can be done for any discipline or topic, but often these are seen in literary research—character or author studies, for example.

History questions will likely involve examination of letters, diaries, and accounts from other primary and secondary sources. Scientific and mathematics studies frequently require generation of data sets from experiment observations, lab reports, and reading the results of other studies on similar questions or topics.

In my experience, most research on the secondary level revolves around social issues. When studying social issues, researchers will almost always find rhetorical pieces of information. To avoid being lured into emotionally charged opinions or, worse, fake news, have students consider whether the social issue is historical in nature (enslavement, immigration, genocide, censorship, bullying, gun control, civil rights, social media, etc.) or scientific in nature (animal rights, weaponry, technology, GMOs, health/nutrition, space, etc.).

This list of social issues is just an example, but it should give us an idea about how to direct students in their quest for potential sources. Any of the topics I listed can be considered from either a scientific or historical viewpoint. Our discipline may dictate the direction, but, ideally, we should give students the choice of what they want to explore. For example, when studying American colonists, a student might choose to examine how animals were treated. Did colonists respect their horses and livestock? How were these animals treated compared with the treatment of the indigenous peoples who populated the land? The information from these questions will not come up on the unit or chapter exam, but to an animal-loving student, they make history come alive. If we are going to assign research so students can learn and "find their own subjects," then we have to allow them to stray from the beaten path a little bit with our guidance and blessing.

We need to help students frame the nature of their inquiries before we set them loose at a computer. Taking the time to think about the direction from which a student is coming at a question, and the type of information they need (books, reports, news items, interviews, case studies, videos, etc.), will set them up for fruitful searches that yield strong material because they will go directly to authoritative sources in formats appropriate to the nature of the search. The following chart illustrates this point. Again, I am using generalization to offer students a place to start thinking about how to categorize the vast amount of information available. I also want to provide them with proper terms for various information formats, a picture of what information looks like, and where to begin looking for it.

| NATURE OF INQUIRY | SOURCES/DATA NEEDED | FORMAT | LOCATION |
|---|---|---|---|
| **Action research, as in SMART goal (see page 24)** | Collect own data set<br><br>Examine writing of authorities on subject | Surveys/logs<br><br>Research studies<br><br>Articles<br><br>Books<br><br>Interviews<br><br>Case studies | Self-generated<br><br>Online databases<br><br>Library<br><br>Periodicals<br><br>Web |
| **Review of literature, as in literary study, author study, character study** | Literary criticism<br><br>Author biographies<br><br>Critical essays<br><br>Authors' own writings about their work(s) | Essays<br><br>Books | Online databases<br><br>Library<br><br>Web |
| **History questions Social issues of a historical nature** | Primary sources: interviews, eyewitness accounts<br><br>Secondary sources: textbooks, edited histories | Books<br><br>Essays and articles<br><br>Regimental registers<br><br>Diaries<br><br>Letters<br><br>Journals<br><br>Photographs<br><br>Case studies<br><br>Opinion/rhetoric | Library<br><br>Online databases<br><br>Web<br><br>Museums<br><br>Historical society collections<br><br>Periodical databases |

| NATURE OF INQUIRY | SOURCES/DATA NEEDED | FORMAT | LOCATION |
|---|---|---|---|
| Science/math questions; social issues of a scientific or mathematical nature | Data set collected from observing experiments<br><br>Proofs<br><br>Biographies<br><br>Previous experiments/ observation | Logs/lab reports<br><br>Books<br><br>Essays and articles<br><br>Scientists' works<br><br>Research studies<br><br>Case studies<br><br>Opinion/rhetoric | Self-generated<br><br>Library<br><br>Online databases<br><br>Web<br><br>Periodical databases |

## Key Search Terms

Once we get students thinking about the various categories and formats of academic information, and we put them on the proper trails, we can begin working on key search terms they can use to locate it. As computer savvy as they are, we cannot assume that students know how to conduct effective online (or offline) searches for information. I often refer to students' Internet search strategies as "The Magic 8-Ball Method." Students go to Google, type a question into the search box—usually the one(s) posed by the teacher on the assignment sheet—and press Enter, hoping for an instant response they can lift.

Key search terms—which can include specialized vocabulary, phrases, names, antonyms, synonyms, and words or phrases that may cover several aspects of the subject—can come from the preliminary reading students did to narrow down the focus of their inquiry and from other thinking they're doing on the subject of study.

As an example, and a model of extending my thinking and connecting prior knowledge, I provided the following lesson to the students I worked with in Freshman Seminar.

### Lesson: Finding Search Terms

My dog, Iggy, is a male pug who weighs about fifteen pounds. He is seven years old, and I strongly suspect he is intelligent. You see, every night Iggy wakes up between 3:00 a.m. and 4:00 a.m. and whines. Because he is unavoidably *my* dog, I get up and let him outside for his constitutional. Since I believe with all my heart that 3:00 a.m. is *way* too early to be active, I then get on the couch and pull a blanket over me, and Iggy and I sleep there until the alarm sounds at a much more decent hour. When I get up, Iggy automatically moves to where my head was on the couch and sits. (See Figure 3.1.) He knows two things: one, I am going to fold up the blanket and return it to its place on the back of the couch, and two, he's about to get his breakfast. Since he wants the second thing to happen as soon as possible, he has learned to get off the blanket quickly.

**Figure 3.1** Iggy waits for breakfast.

Earlier I used the word *intelligent* to describe Iggy, but maybe a better word is *conditioned*. Now, where did this word come from? It came from my prior knowledge. To become an educator, I studied behavioral science a little, and recalling that study, I can see that Iggy is repeating a behavior—well, two behaviors. He gets up at an ungodly hour and then moves out of the way so I can fold the blanket. Because his behavior is the same every time, it may be that he learned it by picking up on cues from what I do:

> He whines at 3:00 a.m.—I get up and let him out of his crate.

> When the alarm rings, I get up (again)—he moves so I can fold the blanket.

Notice that I'm observing something here that is going on in my life, and I have the beginnings of a big question forming. Is Iggy doing what he does because he understands what's happening (which would imply intelligence), or does he do it automatically out of habit (which would imply conditioning)?

To test him, a couple of times I got on the couch without the blanket. Everything else stayed the same: we slept, the alarm went off, and I got up. Lo and behold, Iggy still moved to where my head had been on the couch each time, even though I didn't have to fold up the blanket.

At this point, I begin a class discussion.

"So, if I want to read about this idea before I form a claim, where am I going to look for information that might help me understand what I'm observing with Iggy a little better?"

"Google." (I anticipate this response, so I run with it. I bring up Google on my computer.)

"OK, so then what?"

"Put words in."

"What words?" (Silence while students think. I wait.)

"Dogs?" (I write down *dogs*.)

"OK. What else should I try?"

After another prolonged period of silence, I say, "Well, I used the word *intelligence*, so I'm going to search that, and I also said *conditioning*. If my question goes in the direction I think it's going, I will need to be clear on the meaning of those two words. Let's start there."

I put the word *conditioning* into a Google search box, and I get a definition immediately; I write it down. I scroll down a bit and find a site called Psychologist World, with an article titled "Conditioning," and when I click on it, I come to a page that features a photo of a dog and a trainer. I read the first paragraph aloud and come across the following terms:

| Pavlov | behavioral psychology | response | stimulus |
|--------|----------------------|----------|----------|
| Skinner | classical conditioning | operant conditioning | |

I point out these words and write them in the notes I'm keeping on the board. These are key words—and a jackpot, too! We now know that there are at least two kinds of conditioning, and we can see if Iggy's observed behavior matches either one of those. We also now know that there is such a thing as *behavioral psychology*—there must be a lot of information on that, especially since there are scientists who studied it (whose names we now have as well: Pavlov and Skinner). We can read about their experiments.

I remind students that we have a larger question here than "What is conditioning?" I say, "Now I'm beginning to wonder if conditioning and intelligence are connected in some way. What do I do next?"

"Look up *intelligence*."

"OK."

I do another Google search, plugging in the word *intelligence*. This time I get a definition, which I take down in my notes, but I also come across government-type articles about intelligence: CIA, FBI, and so on. A little more scrolling and there's a tiny bit from *Psychology Today*, which amounts to an expanded definition. There's not much there for search terms—*IQ*, maybe—but now we have a connection: both conditioning and intelligence have something to do with psychology. Further scrolling leads us to *emotional intelligence* and *artificial intelligence*, neither of which is going to help us with this query. We need to keep our reading focused on the question.

I point out to students that now I have some great search terms. I'm going to use a science database to search for information on behavioral science, but *behavioral science* is too broad a term (as is *dogs*), so I will narrow it down to include *conditioning* and *intelligence*, or perhaps the names of the scientists. I will also search the library catalog to see if there are any psychology books or published research studies by Skinner and Pavlov that might be helpful. That is the information I will use to validate my claim:

> Iggy the pug is conditioned to move so I can put away our blanket in the morning. (As an aside, I must also seriously consider the possibility that in fact I am the one who is conditioned here . . .)

There can never be too many search terms in a research plan. It is very helpful for us to model compiling a list of key search terms in class. We can use the method I modeled here, making sure students play a role in the search. In the reflection part at the end of the project, students can go back to their search terms and note which ones rendered the best information. Then they can see the value of forming an organized research plan *before* starting.

Another great way to find key search terms is to do some mind mapping. A mind map is a visual way to get students to think about multiple facets of a given topic, see a direction their thinking is taking them, and perhaps find ideas about what they could search for information. Mind mapping can be extremely useful for developing a big question as well. Figure 3.2 is an example of a mind map using the topic of human cloning.

The mind maps in Figures 3.3 and 3.4 were created by eleventh-grade students who are identical twins. I included these because they are absolutely beautiful examples and they reflect each student's thinking. One began with a big question and worked toward narrowing it down, and the other started with a topic and worked toward a big question. Each mind map gives us insight into the paths the students' thoughts traveled. In Figure 3.3, we can see that the student has a clear understanding of themes in *One Flew Over the Cuckoo's Nest*.

**Figure 3.2** Mind map on human cloning

The other student (Figure 3.4) had a difficult time choosing a direction for her research. Both her teacher and I worked intensively with her to help her along. In the end, she worked it out on her own, which is exactly as it should be.

## The Library: A Real Place to Find Information

Now that we have established that Google is not a place to go for research, we have a research question/claim/thesis/argument, and we have a plan that includes key search terms and various information formats to find, we are ready to dive into research. Our sights now turn to location, location, location.

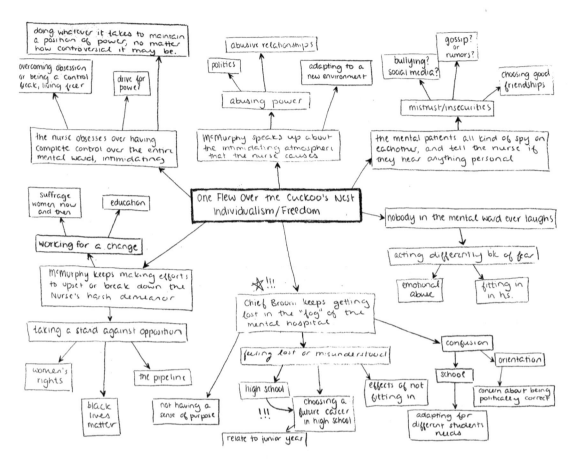

**Figure 3.3** Mind map for *One Flew Over the Cuckoo's Nest*

Libraries contain print materials, of course, but these days you'll also find valuable online resources there, including databases containing scholarly articles, digital versions of reference texts, digital newspapers and magazines, e-books, and much more. The school librarian can acquaint students with these resources. Patrons need not be in the library to access these sources; this can be done from home, from classrooms and computer labs, or from anywhere else an Internet connection exists. If the databases are library subscriptions, patrons will be required to log in with specific usernames and passwords. Again, the librarian can provide these to students and show them how to search the Online Public Access Catalog to find books and other physical or print material right in the library. For more specific information on resources in the library, see Chapter 2.

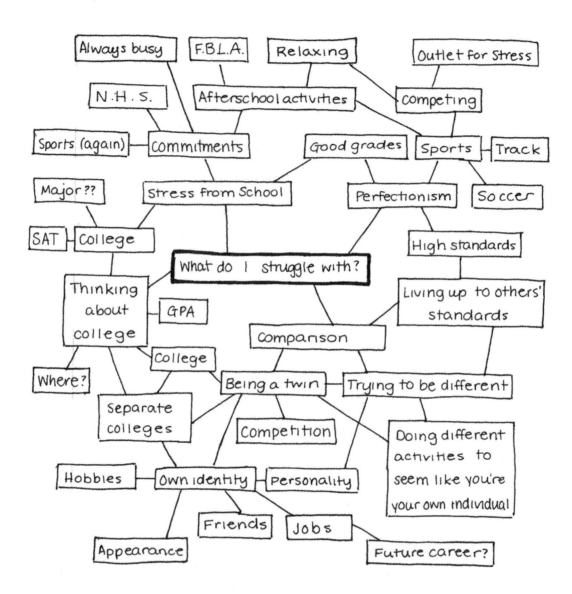

**Figure 3.4** Mind map on "What do I struggle with?"

## Internet Searches

Internet searches may start with Google, but, as discussed earlier in this chapter, there should be a purposeful direction to the search activity. No one should open Google, or any digital database, and put random words in the search box.

Let's return to the cancer inquiry from Chapter 1 and say we want to pursue this question (a compare/contrast, a question of value, a question of relationship):

> *Are older people with cancer treated differently from young people?*

We would have to look at some statistics, determine whether certain cancers afflict people in specific age groups, and find success rates in "curing" childhood versus other cancers. We would have to ask,

> *Who would have this information?*

From my own knowledge, I know that the National Foundation for Cancer Research and the American Cancer Society are good places to look for statistics and studies on different types of cancers and the age groups they affect. Students, who may not have this prior knowledge, will need to think about what institutions could have this information. They could make a list of possible sites and search terms (as I modeled in the lesson on finding search terms on pages 60–61). Students could list major cities that might have research hospitals and find out what they specialize in or use the search term *cancer research hospitals*, which might lead them to the websites of hospitals that specialize in cancer treatment, such as Dana Farber or Dartmouth Hitchcock's Norris Cotton Cancer Center. Personal accounts and case studies of people treated for cancer would be helpful here, as would books on various cancers to learn about the pathology of the disease and possibly its psychological side effects. In this example, both a library and an Internet search could be used to locate the best information for this query. Note that we are identifying the type of information we think we will need to seek out before we start research, and that we are casting a wide net in terms of aspects of the topic: hospital search, personal stories/case studies, pathology, psychological side effects.

Searching within documents is another great way to get to the best sources. Students can use reference lists or Works Cited pages within articles or texts to get to even more authoritative sources. When students do preliminary reading, or start locating information from carefully selected sources, they may start to see the same authors or specific reports/studies cited in several places. Encourage students to pursue access to the reports, authors, or studies they see quoted frequently in their reading, because these are most likely the best authorities on that particular subject.

The point here is to get students into the practice of thinking about the destination (authoritative sources) rather than the hallway they use to get there (Google). The school librarian can be an invaluable resource for us and our students. He or she is there to collaborate with us as we develop research assignments, to assist students with planning their research, and to work with us and our class(es) all the way through to the finish. Too often the librarian is relegated to giving a one-time quick tutorial on the resources, which can be helpful but is not enough to help students develop appropriate research strategies and habits. If there's no librarian at your school, speak to the librarian at the local community library or college/university if there is one nearby.

## Wikipedia: Yes or No?

There has been much debate on the value of Wikipedia as a source of information. Educators, librarians, and college professors question the validity and quality of the information found in its articles. In fact, there is reason for this concern. Tracy Polk, Melissa P. Johnston, and Stephanie Evers conducted a study titled "Wikipedia Use in Research: Perceptions in Secondary Schools," in which they discuss the merits of Wikipedia as a source and, in particular, its article reliability and quality.

> Although the Page Assessment Guide was developed to indicate the quality of an article, in a study done by Lindsey (2010), a frequent contributor to Wikipedia, "nearly one-third of the featured articles assessed were found to fail Wikipedia's own Featured Article criteria" (para. 13). Lindsey randomly selected feature articles and contacted subject experts to evaluate the overall quality of the articles and to compare them against Wikipedia's own criteria for a feature article. Each expert was also asked to rate the article on a scale of one to ten, with ten being the highest rating. Overall, the articles earned an average rating of seven, and of the 22 articles that were assessed, only twelve passed Wikipedia's criteria. (2015, 95)

Besides the fact that the information on Wikipedia's pages can be changed by anyone who has a mind to do it (in fairness, they *have* gotten much better about monitoring the site), the information Wikipedia offers is often factual and encyclopedic. Just as

I would never recommend that students take the entirety of their information from a set of *Encyclopedia Americana,* I would not recommend that students use Wikipedia exclusively. Students love it, though, so I instruct them to use what is in the articles as a way to find more key search terms, or to go straight to the reference list at the bottom of the page. Students can see where the wiki author gathered his or her information, and instead of using the potentially unreliable information in the wiki itself, they can go directly to more authoritative sources. In other words, Wikipedia is most effective as a starting point for research—to address the "what" question(s).

## A Sidebar on Print

There are a lot of good reasons print material remains viable and valuable as a resource for secondary students' research. In fact, it can be used to great effect in students' initial foray into locating, evaluating, and using information. Modeling how to locate information can be done using books, which have two "search engines": the table of contents and the index. Key search terms can be generated using a book's index, and evaluation/assessment of relevance to the research question can be determined by using the table of contents.

Close reading can be done by extracting material from a book and annotating it, questioning it, and looking at the references or bibliography. A book may also contain aspects of a given topic that can be pursued as alternate directions of inquiry. Librarians and teachers can demonstrate all of this *before* students are set loose on the Internet.

Print material has other benefits too, such as the very reassuring fact that the information contained therein has been vetted by at least an editor and possibly peer review. Print is reliable because it is unalterable; any alterations to it are easily detectable and discreditable. Print lacks the distraction factor that an open Google search brings. By its nature, a book contains only what it says it contains. It can lead readers to other places, but they have to willfully go there, and it takes more effort than a click. Print has the potential to be biased, as any online source does, which is a lesson in itself. (More on this in Chapter 7.)

Print is a great way for students to get physical with information. They have to handle and flip the pages as they read, hold it in their hands. Print is real, and it's easier to see that it is a force to be reckoned with. A reader feels a closer connection to the author when reading print as well (see Chapter 4).

## Information Literacy

The Association of College and Research Libraries defines *information literacy* as follows:

> Information literacy is the set of integrated abilities encompassing the reflective discovery of information, the understanding of how information is produced and valued, and the use of information in creating new knowledge and participating ethically in communities of learning. (2015)

This concise definition encompasses a wide range of skills, up to and including critical and higher-order thinking. Research projects are the ultimate way to apply these important skills, plus a few others such as decoding and encoding (otherwise known as reading and writing). Trouble arises because research demands a high level of ability in locating, accessing, assessing, absorbing, parsing, ruminating, synthesizing, and finally creating a product that exhibits discovery, critical judgment, and new knowledge in a cogent and academically acceptable way, all the while being respectful of the information it took to build the new knowledge and the people who produced it. None of this is easy, but it's definitely worth the ride. Be prepared for the fact that the research process casts a rather large spotlight on deficiencies in reading and writing of nonfiction texts, both of which require time for thinking. (See Chapter 4.)

We all must cover specified and proscribed volumes of content and then assess whether students have retained it—it's an endless merry-go-round. When do students get to work on understanding? Often, it's not until college (if they go), when learning the content of their course curricula is almost entirely turned over to them.

College students are required to do the professor-selected course reading, wrestle with it, and then come to class prepared to discuss it—if they're lucky. Often, college professors eschew open discussions in favor of lecture during class meetings, which results in more content that has to be mulled over and evaluated against the course readings. To be prepared for this style of learning, college students have to be proficient in close reading and note-taking, and they must know who they are as learners. A study conducted by Regional Educational Laboratory Southwest found that "about half of public school students in grade 11 in Texas are prepared to read at the University of Texas system. At the 75 percent comprehension level, 51 percent are able to read and comprehend 95 percent of the textbooks used in entry-level English courses; 80 percent

are able to read and comprehend 50 percent of the textbooks; and 9 percent are able
to read no more than 5 percent of the textbooks" (Wilkins et al. 2012, 10). As someone
who was underprepared for college myself, I can tell you it is a rude awakening. A good
percentage of students fail to clear the bar. They are unaccustomed to this level of rigor,
and some of them lack the personal fortitude to persevere. A lot of money is wasted, and
what do they take from the experience? Failure. Six months later, the student loans are
due. (*Shudder.*) Let's go back to high school . . .

## Moving Past Surface-Level Thinking: Evaluating Resources

The overabundance of information accessible today makes it necessary—imperative,
even—that students learn how to evaluate the quality and relevance of information as it
pertains to their research question. To help students manage and navigate vast amounts
of information, school librarians instruct them on how to evaluate Internet sources
using specific criteria with memorable initialisms and acronyms, such as the ABCDs of
Website Evaluation:

> A – Author
>
> B – Bias
>
> C – Content
>
> D – Date

Or, my personal favorite, the CRAAP Test (O'Connor et al. 2010, 228):

> C – Currency
> R – Relevance
> A – Authority
> A – Accuracy
> P – Purpose

The intent behind this instruction is basically good. Because literally anyone can post
information on the World Wide Web, we want students to avoid falling prey to dated,
blatantly biased information rife with inaccuracies churned out by unauthoritative
figures (now known as "fake news"). It seems like a good idea to give students a set of
guidelines they can easily remember so they can assess whether a piece of information

is worth including in their research. Practitioners have studied this method and found that, although it may help students eliminate dated or unauthoritative material, it also reinforces surface-level consideration because students cling to criteria like they're a life raft. These evaluation methods have become another crutch, much like the five-paragraph essay.

O'Connor et al. report that "Workshop instructors found most students were concerned more about assessing 'checklist criteria' than the site's content or message. Students focused on superficial features of information sources rather than on actually using information to develop a greater understanding of a topic'" (2010, 229).

In the balance, it is far more important that students absorb and judge the actual content of the information than it is to eliminate it for "superficial" reasons. If we take the time to allow students to acquire background or "working knowledge" (Ballenger 2015, 32), and we encourage them to be thoughtful about which key search terms and what sites, sources, and formats they will use to locate good information, the need for "checklist criteria" when evaluating sources will be virtually eliminated.

When students consider a question or problem for study, taking time to find out who has studied the same problem can help them locate the best source(s) because they will be going directly to an authority on the subject. For example, Ozzy Osbourne is not an authority on astrophysics; therefore anything he has written on the subject would have to be questioned for accuracy. Osbourne does have quite an impressive body of work as an entertainer and musician to his name. I would trust anything he has said or written on that subject implicitly.

Planning for research as a strategy is far superior to sitting at a computer and leaving it to chance (or Google). People who have done a body of work or study on a subject make sure their names are attached to it. As a general rule, students should avoid using information with no apparent author or corporate sponsor listed. Once the preliminary groundwork has been done, the evaluation piece then becomes a matter of determining whether conflicting information or results exist, making sure the information accessed is the most current and accurate available, and checking for relevance to the original research question. Students will need to be able to read and digest carefully the information they locate. (More on evaluating sources in Chapter 7.)

### A Note on Organization

Students in the throes of research projects must keep everything in some order and ideally in one place. I recommend plain manila folders with headings like "Sources," "Notes and Annotations," and "Reference List/Works Cited/Bibliography." Students will also need access to highlighters, staplers, pens, lined paper or a notebook, sticky notes, paper clips, and index cards.

Digital tools are available—Microsoft's OneNote, for example—that simulate paper items such as sticky notes or note cards and can be used to great effect as well. Research shows that secondary students have very little practice grappling with informational texts, and people do not read well on screens. (See Chapter 4 for more on reading.)

Until we are convinced that students can handle academic material, I recommend that they print or photocopy the information they will use so they can physically work with it away from the distraction of screens.

Yes, this is an old-fashioned method—but students need to learn how to wrestle with informational texts, and research shows that this is best accomplished with pen and paper.

## Note-Taking

Students need a lot of practice with reacting to information they receive from nonfiction texts. If they are to judge nonfiction texts for accuracy and relevance with an analytical eye, they must become highly proficient at close reading and taking notes.

We can model both close reading and note-taking skills in class by starting a discussion on a shared piece of informational reading. Then we can demonstrate annotating the piece by displaying the collected thinking and reactions of the class on the board or using a document camera. (Remember, even though we may not see teaching reading as part of our skill set, we are the most knowledgeable about our particular discipline in the classroom and are therefore the best person to guide students through readings from our field. Think of how we read as a scientist, mathematician, or historian.) Here are some questions you might use to begin a discussion on an informational piece:

Does the author present both sides of the issue?

Are there references at the end of the piece?

Who is the intended audience, and how do you know?

Does the piece raise more questions for us?

Is the information presented relevant to the inquiry or research question?

Are there words, phrases, or names in the article that could be used as key search terms to find additional information?

Does the piece open your eyes to different ways of looking at the subject of study?

What did you learn from reading the piece that you didn't know before you read it?

Do you agree with the conclusions/findings/information the author presented?

When we are ready to allow students to try reacting to their reading on their own, double-entry journals can be used to great effect (Ballenger 2015). To set up a double-entry journal, we simply take a piece of white lined paper and fold it lengthwise (or create a document in Word with two columns, or use opposite pages in a notebook; see Figure 3.5. Alternatively, students can use the Reaction to Resources organizer shown in Figures 3.6 and 3.7, which will guide their responses as a scaffold). On top of the journal page, we write the citation for the source with which we're working. On the left side, we write any paraphrases, direct quotations, and summaries we took from the source. Be sure to include page numbers for each one. On the right side, we react to each paraphrase, quote, and summary by applying the preceding questions. We can add these questions suggested by Ballenger as well:

What strikes you? What is confusing? What is surprising?

If you assume that this is true, why is it significant?

If you doubt the truth or accuracy of the claim or fact, what is the author failing to consider?

How does the information stand up to your own experiences and observations?

Does it support or contradict your thesis/claim (if you have one at this point)?

How might you use the information in your paper? What purpose might it serve?

What do you think of the source?

How does the information connect to the other sources you've read?
(2015, 124–125)

## Double–Entry Journal

Fraser

Source Citation: _____

| What the Text Said: | What I Say: |
| --- | --- |
| | |

Figure 3.5 Double-entry journal

Reaction to Resources

Name:_____            Print                    Online

Source Citation: _____
_____

Does the author present both sides of the issue?        Yes        No
Are there references at the end of the piece?           Yes        No

Who is the intended audience and how do you know? _____
_____

Is the information presented relevant to the inquiry/topic?   Yes        No

Are there words, phrases, or names in the article that could be used as key search terms to find
additional information?

They are:        _____        _____

                 _____        _____

Does the piece open your eyes to different ways of looking at the subject?  Yes        No

How so? What did you learn?_____
_____
_____
_____
_____
_____

Do you agree with the conclusions the author presented?     Yes        No

Why or why not? _____
_____

Does the piece raise more questions for you?            Yes        No

What are your questions? _____
_____
_____

**Figure 3.6** Blank Reaction to Resources organizer

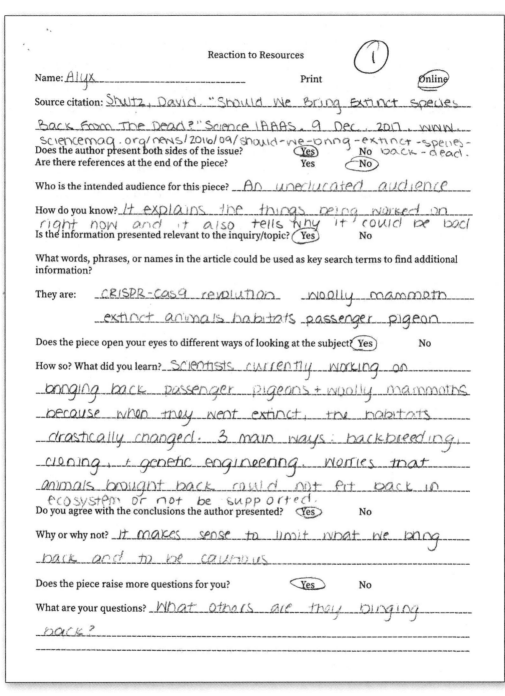

**Reaction to Resources** ①

Name: Alyx _____     Print          Online

Source citation: Shutz, David. "Should We Bring Extinct Species Back From The Dead?" Science IAAAS, 9 Dec. 2017. www. sciencemag.org/news/2016/09/should-we-bring-extinct-species-back-dead.

Does the author present both sides of the issue?          Yes          No

Are there references at the end of the piece?          Yes          No

Who is the intended audience for this piece? An uneducated audience

How do you know? It explains the things being worked on right now and it also tells why it could be bad

Is the information presented relevant to the inquiry/topic? Yes          No

What words, phrases, or names in the article could be used as key search terms to find additional information?

They are: CRISPR-cas9 revolution   woolly mammoth extinct animals habitats passenger pigeon

Does the piece open your eyes to different ways of looking at the subject? Yes          No

How so? What did you learn? Scientists currently working on bringing back passenger pigeons + woolly mammoths because when they went extinct, the habitats drastically changed. 3 main ways: backbreeding, cloning, + genetic engineering. Worries that animals brought back could not fit back in ecosystem or not be supported.

Do you agree with the conclusions the author presented? Yes          No

Why or why not? It makes sense to limit what we bring back and to be cautious

Does the piece raise more questions for you?          Yes          No

What are your questions? What others are they bringing back?

**Figure 3.7** Student example of the Reaction to Resources organizer

Being organized note-takers is going to be key for students' success in evaluating information and putting it all together to discover something unknown. Research builds knowledge. Scaffolding will be needed for high school students initially. If students see these information literacy skills repeated in every discipline a couple of times per year, they will become familiar with the work and the scaffolding can fall away. Building these skills is a process.

Figure 3.8 shows a notes organizer that I developed for students to take notes by hand. (I borrowed some ideas from *Reading Nonfiction* by Kylene Beers and Robert Probst [2016].) Figure 3.9 provides examples of students' notes using a digitized version of this form.

These students are doing much more with the information from the source than copying it verbatim. Real thinking is evident in their notes.

**Information Search Organizer**

Name _____ Source type:  ☐ Online  ☐ Print

Fraser

Source Citation: _____

| Search Terms Used: | Notes from source including quotes and graphics: |
| --- | --- |

What surprised me? _____

What did the author already think I knew? _____

What changed, challenged, or confirmed what I already knew? (Beers & Probst, 2016, p. 76) _____

Beers, K. & Probst, R. (2016). *Reading Nonfiction: Notice & Note Stances, Signposts, and Strategies*. Portsmouth, NH: Heinemann.

**Figure 3.8** Information Search Organizer

# Information Search Organizer

| Source Type (print or online) | Search Terms Used |
| --- | --- |
| Online | Desegregation in schools |

**Source Citation**

"Desegregation, School." International Encyclopedia of the Social Sciences, edited by William A. Darity, Jr., 2nd ed., vol. 2, Macmillan Reference USA, 2008, pp. 316-319. U.S. History in Context, link.galegroup.com/apps/doc/CX3045300566/UHIC?u=nhais_hdpm&xid=d2f0e8ac. Accessed 15 Mar. 2017.

**Notes from Source (including quotes and graphics)**

In 1954 brown vs board of edu. case ruled that desegregation was a violation of the 14th amendment. "It was a promise to America's black children of an education available to all on equal terms with that given to whites" Chief Justice Earl Warren Federal support for desegregation was appointed. "Minority segregation in education can be attributed to self-segregation in housing by minorities. This is particularly true for recent immigrants who often find it easier to adjust to life in the United States when surrounded by people who are culturally similar." (Connection to common day immigration problems).

**What surprised me?**                                      (Beers & Probst, 2016, p. 76)

Since the early 1990's school segregation is increasing rather than decreasing. Segregation is often the result of segregation in housing.

**What did the author already think I knew?**              (Beers & Probst, 2016, p. 76)

The history of how equal rights came to be through various court cases such as Brown Vs. Education of Topeka.

**What changed, challenged, or confirmed what I already knew?**   (Beers & Probst, 2016, p. 76)

In the 1980's some American school in many areas remained starkly segregated. Many schools fell back into segregation when Ronald Reagan's term expired.

**Figure 3.9** Student examples of the Information Search Organizer

# Information Search Organizer

| Source Type (print or online) | Search Terms Used |
|---|---|
| Online | Great Depression |

| Source Citation |
|---|
| "Great Depression." *Gale Encyclopedia of U.S. Economic History*, edited by Thomas Carson and Mary Bonk, Gale, 1999. *U.S. History in Context*, link.galegroup.com/apps/doc/EJ1667500277/UHIC?u=nhais_hdpm&xid=739cb087. Accessed 13 Mar. 2017. |

### Notes from Source (including quotes and graphics)

- Stock market crashed on October 29, 1929
- The Great Depression is the longest and darkest depression ever in American History
- Industrial Production fell 51% before slightly improving in 1932
- Nearly 1.5 million people in the country without jobs before the Great Depression, nearly an estimated amount of 16 million people unemployed at the peak of the Great Depression

### What surprised me?

- Farmers may have been the economic group that was hit the hardest during the Great Depression- their total combined income drop from $11.9 billion to $5.3 billion
- President Herbert Hoover (1929-1933) created the Reconstruction Finance Corporation (RFC), which was a loan agency designed to help large business concerns, including banks, railroads, and insurance companies
- Hoover was granted funds from Congress to cut down the number of farm foreclosures
- Hoover also signed a relief bill incomparable to anything in American history. "The Emergency Relief and Construction Act provided $300 million for local relief loans and $1.5 billion for self-liquidating public works"
- By 1937, America was starting to make a comeback from the Great Depression, some of which were almost equal to their stats before the crash of the Stock Market
- Unemployment was still around 7.5 million people, even after the Great Depression

### What did the author already think I knew/what confused me?

- Where did the money for the relief bill that Hoover signed come from? $1.8 billion is a lot of money, especially during the Great Depression, one of the lowest points in American History, so how could the country afford giving away $1.8 billion?

### What changed, challenged, or confirmed what I already knew?

- The date/event of the crash of the Stock Market confirmed that I already knew when it occurred, and that it caused the Great Depression.
- Unemployment rates increased dramatically during the Great Depression

**Figure 3.9** Student examples of the Information Search Organizer (continued)

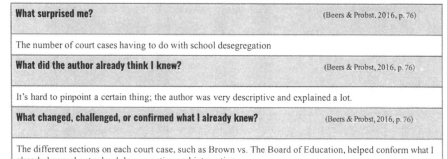

## Information Search Organizer

| Source Type (print or online) | Search Terms Used |
|---|---|
| Online | School Segregation; Segregation in Schools |

| Source Citation |
|---|
| "Education Rights." *Civil Rights in America: 1500 to the present*, edited by Jay A. Sigler, Gale, 1998. *U.S. History in Context*, link.galegroup.com/apps/doc/BT2302200012/UHIC?u=nhais_hdpm&xid=0ee2bc8c. Accessed 10 Mar. 2017. |

| Notes from Source (including quotes and graphics) |
|---|
| - "Many claim that the challenge of the twenty-first century will be crossing color and class borders"<br>- Brown vs. board of ed. And Brown 2 both involved several community efforts by African-American students and parents to cross racial border and integrate the public schools of their respective communities.<br>- "Every public school district with black and white student populations and legal segregation had to provide equal education opportunities for all children<br>- School systems and federal district judges relied on the expertise and recommendations of social scientists and educators trained to address efforts of desegregation and integration |

| What surprised me? | (Beers & Probst, 2016, p. 76) |
|---|---|

| The number of court cases having to do with school desegregation |
|---|

| What did the author already think I knew? | (Beers & Probst, 2016, p. 76) |
|---|---|

| It's hard to pinpoint a certain thing; the author was very descriptive and explained a lot. |
|---|

| What changed, challenged, or confirmed what I already knew? | (Beers & Probst, 2016, p. 76) |
|---|---|

| The different sections on each court case, such as Brown vs. The Board of Education, helped conform what I already knew about school desegregation and integration. |
|---|

**Figure 3.9** Student examples of the Information Search Organizer (continued)

# Chapter 4

## The Importance of Strong Comprehension Skills in Research

*You'll never achieve 100 percent if 99 percent is okay.*

—Will Smith

When I was in sixth grade, I had an educational epiphany of sorts. Of course, I only know this now because it's forty years later and I have the benefit of perspective. At the time, I felt it more as an inconvenience.

My teacher was a tiny but formidable woman who'd been married three times, as the rumor went. She wore skirts, blouses, wool blazers, and a dour expression every day. There was not an ounce of fat on her. Her hair was dyed a deep brown and teased up for height. A line at her throat marked the edge of foundation makeup two shades darker than her natural complexion. She was probably not much older than I am now.

I was terrified of her.

In the spring, she assigned us a biography book report. We were to select a biography of a famous American, read it, and write a short paper on what we learned. Although I can't recall for sure, I doubt there were questions or prompts provided to guide us in this endeavor. I ended up with a biography of Brigham Young. To say that I was uninspired by this assignment is to understate the situation completely. I didn't read the book at all.

The night before the report was due, I cast about desperately trying to find something to put down on paper. At the end of the book I found a bulleted list of facts about Mr. Young, which I copied longhand, verbatim, and with no transitions. This I submitted as my own completed work.

Not long afterward, the teacher called me to her desk. She had my paper in her hand. Without preamble she said, "You didn't read this book, did you?"

"No."

"Why not?"

"I don't like the book."

"Find a biography you will read and do this over. You have a week."

I received no lecture on plagiarism. She did not express disappointment, nor did she threaten me with a penalty for resubmitting the assignment. From the town library I checked out *Julia Ward Howe: Girl of Old New York* by Jean Brown Wagoner and read it cover to cover. I can still remember the story of Julia Ward Howe's life of privilege in New York City, how she lost her mother early due to complications of childbirth, that she wrote "Battle Hymn of the Republic" and lived to be ninety-one years old.

I have also thought about the pedagogical brilliance of that exchange many, many times. My teacher held me accountable for the reading and work without making me feel bad about it (although I will admit to a little fear and embarrassment), and, best of all, she didn't tell my parents. I benefited from actually doing the reading, which she knew I would.

The importance of students' ability to read competently cannot be overemphasized. Once people leave formal schooling, one of the primary ways they learn is by reading. The written word is the major mode of communication in almost every aspect of life and in just about every medium.

In this chapter, we are going to look at analysis, synthesis, and reflection—the last, and arguably most challenging, parts of the research process. These parts are the scary ones for both students and us. Students fear being wrong in their thinking, a result of the question-answer notion of "research." They have told me they will change their thesis statement or experiment results before they will write about how what they read or observed differed from their predictions, beliefs, and thinking. Students don't like academic surprises or the possibility of failure, so when they learn that their guess is off the mark, they revert to compliance mode and "change" their argument to fall in line with the prevailing tides. They abandon their voice. They roll over. No grit. No growth.

Analysis is another piece missing from high school students' research projects, because often students are not pushed to go beyond the "what" questions. If we ask "what" and they answer it, they usually think they're done. There's no scope for analysis in some of our assignments. We fear analysis and synthesis because they require students to take some steps away from our direct instruction and to make their own connections, which we then have to assess. Responding to students' discoveries takes a lot more time, thought, and effort than checking their work for content does. (These concerns are valid and understandable, but for now, I'm going to leave the subject of assessment. We will look at it in depth in Chapter 6.) Reading and writing are not exclusive to the English language arts department. They never were. We must put aside our own worry and reluctance and learn to consider students as both writers and creators of knowledge. We can read and respond to their work in the same way we read and respond to the authors in our field and discipline. Further, as I mentioned earlier, we must teach students how to make meaning of the complex informational texts written about subjects in our disciplines.

Before students can analyze, they must be able to read, draw meaning from, and internalize the information they locate. In the next few pages, we are going to look at reading in greater depth, but we will also touch on other literacies: disciplinary literacy, information literacy, and data literacy.

## Comprehension Is Critical

I am the librarian at a midsized high school in rural New Hampshire. About ten years ago, I attended a department chair meeting at which we discussed the disappointing writing scores on the NHEAP test. At that time, I thought, *This isn't a writing problem. This is a reading problem.* That thought stayed with me for a while. I also thought someone should do something about it. A couple years later I decided that *I* was someone, so, with the full support of my administrators, I went back to school.

These days it appears students are reading more than ever, which should be a positive thing, but test scores indicate otherwise. In fact, the numbers are dismal. More than a quarter of the nation's eighth-grade students read below basic level, and only about one-third of eighth graders read at a proficient level. When we examine the data for twelfth graders, we find that reading achievement among this group has *declined* since 2002, and a mere one-third of all high school graduates are able to handle academic reading for college (Leko and Mundy 2012; Paige, Rasinski, and Magpuri-Lavell 2012).

In most high schools you won't find a reading specialist or literacy coach, but it is increasingly clear that there is a need for one or both to serve not only students but also teachers. I say it's increasingly clear because the Common Core State Standards (CCSS) focus heavily on the reading of informational texts, particularly in the content-area disciplines. Since the standards call for all teachers to focus on literacy, now is the time to examine how we are instructing our students in the readings unique to our study.

In earlier chapters I mentioned disciplinary literacy, and reading is an important place to apply it. Students may encounter academic or content-specific vocabulary and even differences in syntax when reading scholarly journal articles and other informational texts while conducting research (Fang and Pace 2013; Fang and Schleppegrell 2010; Frey and Fisher 2013; Beers and Probst 2016). The language and structure of academic material have challenged many students, because this kind of writing is deliberately and markedly different from the writing they are accustomed to in novels, or even editorials, which may be filled with literary devices such as metaphor and figurative language. There the sentence structure is relatively simple, especially in the age-appropriate young adult fiction high school students most often read. Academic writing requires close reading and work on the part of the reader to make meaning of it.

## Complex, Discipline-Specific Language and Texts

Students need rigor and perseverance to interpret complex texts before they can use them to support a claim or thesis. Merely "reading" to the end of an article isn't going to cut it. They have to wrestle with the material. They have to employ reading strategies to develop their skills in understanding complex texts. "Close reading is called for in the CCSS" (Fang and Pace 2013, 106).

Much has been written about instructing and advancing students' skills in reading and understanding informational texts. We cannot assume that high school students—even upperclassmen in Advanced Placement courses—know how to extract meaning from academic material. If a piece seems too dense, it's likely they will reject it for one that contains surface factual information. (This is an unpleasant by-product of nearly two decades on a steady diet of No Child Left Behind [Gallagher 2015].)

Secondary students may lack the background knowledge to recognize or understand references to other studies or aspects of a subject. They might not have encountered much of the specialized vocabulary, and the sheer number and placement of clauses in academic writing can throw off their understanding completely. The rest of us experience these difficulties with complex texts as well, but we know we must take the time to look up unfamiliar references and vocabulary; seek relational evidence in the text; question what we're reading; weigh the information against the claim, thesis, or research question; and annotate passages that are confusing to us in order to hold meaning. We know that it is work to wrest understanding and relevance from information, and that this work is best done away from a computer screen. Most of our students will not even attempt to read an article that is more than five pages long.

The sources I consulted recommend that teachers model close reading strategies for complex texts in their disciplines for their students using a think-aloud method. We can show students our process for making meaning from a chunk of discipline-specific text. Scaffolding is another recommendation, but take care to avoid doing too much of the work. We need to gradually release responsibility for learning to our students. Frey and Fisher caution against too much scaffolding or too little instruction:

> To ensure that students actually do learn to read complex texts, teachers have to scaffold instruction and know when to transfer the cognitive and metacognitive responsibility to students. They need to rethink the texts they use, expanding the range to include more complex texts accompanied by scaffolds and support. And they need to carefully consider the intentional instruction students need to receive if they are going to apply what they have learned to the wide world of texts available to them. (2013, 2)

## Reading Strategies: Making Thinking Visible

Helping students see their thinking while they read can boost their confidence and provide a much more productive experience when tackling nonfiction texts. Making thinking visible is part of close reading and can be done in several ways.

Cris Tovani (2004) suggests we provide explicit instruction on how to mark up a text or article. Exercises can be done as a whole class with the teacher modeling the activities, or in pairs of students, or individually. As with other skills, the teacher should gradually release the responsibility for learning to students.

The goal is to show students that readers of informational texts are active learners and, as such, are engaged in several learning strategies. Tovani lists the following activities students can do while reading a complex text:

- Write thinking in the margins or on sticky notes next to the words or ideas that caused them to have a thought. Underline those words and ideas in the text.

- Respond to text as if they're having a conversation with the author about it, rather than simply copying the text.

- Ask a question, make a connection to something they know, give an opinion, draw a conclusion, make a statement. (2004, 69)

Students can also make note of references and terms they don't know or understand and either look for clarifying information or ask about them in class discussion. Everyone benefits from these clarifications and connections.

Beers and Probst suggest that it's "the reader's responsibility to question his or her own beliefs and assumptions while struggling with determining what's true—or not— in the text" (2016, 19). Nonfiction is "messy" because it contains theories, philosophies, general knowledge, histories, and so on. Authors are human, and they carry their perceptions, perspectives, and biases into what they write. Think about the function of rhetoric, or scientific writing—both of which strive to persuade or to prove a point or theory. Even history can be presented differently, depending on the region in which it is being taught. "Much of our job in reading nonfiction is to evaluate what the author has done in the text" (Beers and Probst 2016, 21).

Most of us were not trained in college to teach reading. No one expects us to be expert reading teachers, but because we're the experts on our discipline in the room, the task falls to us to guide students through reading the informational texts in our content areas. Following are some excellent resources to help with teaching reading strategies in different disciplines. Even adopting one or two strategies will help us guide our students in reading complex texts.

### Resources to Help Students Read Texts in Your Discipline

There are some excellent resources for helping content-area teachers teach students how to make meaning of nonfiction texts, most notably:

*Do I Really Have to Teach Reading? Content Comprehension, Grades 6-12* by Cris Tovani

Tovani's approach is focused more on readers' responses to texts and holding meaning.

*Reading Nonfiction: Notice & Note Stances, Signposts, and Strategies* by Kylene Beers and Robert E. Probst

*Diving Deep into Nonfiction: Transferable Tools for Reading* Any *Nonfiction Text, Grades 6-12* by Jeffrey D. Wilhelm and Michael W. Smith

Both Beers and Probst and Wilhelm and Smith recommend strategies that teach students to pay attention not only to what's in the text but also to how the text is structured. Beers and Probst call the features and structure of the text "signposts," whereas Wilhelm and Smith use the phrase "rules of notice for text structure" (2017, 170).

*Reading in Secondary Content Areas: A Language-Based Pedagogy* by Zhihui Fang and Mary J. Schleppegrell

Fang and Schleppegrell have conducted many studies on literacy with informational texts, and this slim volume contains information on how to identify the specific characteristics of science, math, history or social studies, and language arts texts. They say that in science texts, for example, the language is typically "technical," "abstract," "dense," and "tightly knit" (2008, 21-37). As such, teachers must provide students with explicit instruction in making meaning when reading texts with those characteristics.

Language in history texts can be analyzed by asking three questions: "How did the author organize this section? What is going on in the text? What is the perspective of the author?" (Fang and Schleppegrell 2008, 43). Beers and Probst (2016) suggest the "Somebody Wanted But So" (SWBS) strategy. SWBS is a summarizing strategy developed by James Macon, Diane Bewell, and MaryEllen Vogt that helps students zero in on important points instead of rehashing large chunks of text. It is a handy tool for students and can be used to summarize history texts as well as fiction. For example: **_The Colonists_** *(S)* **_wanted_** *(W) to be free of what they thought were tyrannical taxes and other actions by King George III* **_but_** *(B) he refused to listen to their side of the argument,* **_so_** *(S) they declared their intention to gain independence from the crown.*

*This Is Disciplinary Literacy: Reading, Writing, Thinking, and Doing . . . Content Area by Content Area* by Releah Cossett Lent

Lent's book "zeroes in on the academic habits that matter most" in your specific discipline and shows what implementing strategies looks like in the classroom. She addresses responding to and giving feedback on students' writing.

All of these sources make great use of questioning as a strategy that good readers use to make meaning of nonfiction texts.

These strategies can be used for working with informational texts in any discipline. It will also be helpful for students to know the language and characteristics of discipline-specific texts.

Please see your school librarian or reading specialist for more resources on teaching reading strategies specific to the writing and texts in your discipline.

As I mentioned in Chapter 3, no student should be set loose on the Internet without a plan or the strategies he or she needs to locate, access, and use high-quality information. The information students use for research can be in the form of charts, diagrams, architectural schematics, maps, graphs, music, and artifacts, as well as photographs, videos, and cartoons, all of which require specific reading strategies that are different from reading literary texts and fall under the heading of *data literacy*. Then there is the discipline-specific vocabulary of science, history, and math. Students must understand the "form and function" (Coffin 2006, 39) of various discipline-specific texts if they are to use them effectively to create new knowledge.

It takes a lot of practice before one can produce a presentation or piece of writing that seamlessly incorporates one's thinking on a subject of study with evidence gathered from various authorities on that topic. We have to help students see that, to use information properly, they must understand it, assess its relevance to their own thinking (claim, thesis, question), mark their discoveries, and give credit to the authors and creators of the information as they use it in their final presentation. The goal of research is always to "discover [something] that we don't already know" (Ballenger 2015, xxii). The skills needed for real learning are a long way from Google→copy→paste→done.

## Computers and Reading

One of the problems students have with academic reading is that many of them lack stamina—that is, they don't read for prolonged periods. They read in short bursts, which does not build reading fluency, increase vocabulary and comprehension, allow them to grapple with big questions, or encourage empathy. By its nature, online reading seems to exacerbate the stamina problem.

Please understand that I am not against technology. We are living in a time of unparalleled access to a breathtaking array of information, and this access is a great development for the human race. My concerns about thrusting students into this environment unprepared, however, are profound. Imagine a family—parents and two children, for example—all holding hands before the wrought-iron gates of a zoo. In time, the gates swing open. The parents let go of the children's hands, and they run in headlong without supervision. Students unsupervised on the open Internet are in as dangerous a situation as children set loose alone in the zoo.

I hope this metaphor sticks with you. If students do not know how to read critically, their time on the computer is not going to help them improve this skill. In fact, the opposite is true. The Internet, for better or worse, is most students' resource of choice, and it is set up like a multilayered marketplace that includes carnival-like visual barkers and lots of flash. It is designed to put endless info-bits in front of consumers, tailored to their particular tastes and desires, as quickly as possible. Students often display remarkable agility in manipulating the keyboard, and we equate this prowess with literacy. The truth is that our students must be adept at reading and thinking critically or they risk being consumed in the lion's cage, much like unsupervised children at the zoo.

Some theorize that adolescent literacy has suffered greatly at the hands of technology.

We are already seeing that students have difficulty with discourse and critical thinking on college campuses. Mark Bauerlein devotes an entire chapter to this idea in his controversial book *The Dumbest Generation: How the Digital Age Stupefies Young Americans and Jeopardizes Our Future [or, Don't Trust Anyone Under 30]*. He posits that there is a direct correlation between decreasing test scores and diminished reading time among high school students. He cites Jakob Nielsen and Don Norman, whose work in the 1990s spawned the sharp, eye-catching graphics and web page "usability" we now enjoy (2008, 142). They studied the behavior of subjects reading online by tracking eye movements. Nielsen and Norman used these data to advise their heavy-hitter clients on how to construct web page designs to increase marketing and sales. In the process, they discovered information that has serious implications for literacy.

> Using the eyetracker in successive studies from the early 1990s through 2006, Nielsen has reached a set of conclusions regarding how users take in text as they go online and browse, and they demonstrate that screen reading differs greatly from book reading. In 1997, he issued an alert entitled, "How Users Read on the Web." The first sentence ran, "They don't" (emphasis in original). Only 16 percent of the subjects read text on various pages linearly, word by word and sentence by sentence. The rest scanned the pages, "picking out individual words and sentences," processing them out of sequence. The eyetracker showed users jumping around, fixating on pieces that interest them and passing over the rest. This is what the screen encourages users to do, Nielsen observes. (Bauerlein 2008, 143)

Indeed, there is a scientific explanation for why text on paper is absorbed better by humans. Our minds *map* text on a page, as opposed to merely scanning it as they do on a screen. "Beyond treating individual letters as physical objects, the human brain may also perceive a text in its entirety as a kind of physical landscape. When we read, we construct a mental representation of the text. The exact nature of such representations remains unclear, but some researchers think they are similar to the mental maps we create of terrain—such as mountains and trails—and of indoor physical places, such as apartments and offices" (Jabr 2013). This idea makes sense. When flipping pages to locate information in a book, the eye goes to each of the quadrants on the two pages in a *Z* motion: upper-left-to-upper-right-to-bottom-left-to-bottom-right. People can often remember the approximate physical location of the information they're looking for on the page. That kind of muscle memory, if you will, is not possible when scrolling through an online document.

There are other compelling reasons why ensuring that students are actually reading texts is so important. Bauerlein also cites a study in which Anne E. Cunningham and Keith E. Stanovich analyze the occurrence of rare words in various places that might appear in children's environments, such as television, print materials, and adult speech. Hands down, print materials present the greatest opportunity for students to encounter rare words, which helps increase vocabulary and, subsequently, comprehension (1998).

One of our goals as educators is to help students with language acquisition, and the best way for us to do that is to expose them to complete texts. Research is a great way to have students grapple with complex, discipline-specific texts. The problem is, we don't compel them to read widely and deeply during the research process. We turn them loose in the computer lab, where they fall into their established pattern of clicking around, scanning sites for info bites, copying, and pasting.

Research projects are also a tremendous opportunity for students to practice critical-thinking skills, but in order to get authentic experience in developing as deep thinkers, they must spend *time* with a subject/issue/question/topic. Computers are an incredible tool, but the way they're being used by students in school runs counter to critical thinking. Students can't give proper thought to an idea or a question if they're skimming the reading at breakneck speed. Students need to consider all sides, question an issue, read long works, and write more than two pages.

Another benefit of having students step back from the computer is "the pause"—a phenomenon Thomas Friedman (2016) mentions in his book *Thank You for Being Late: An Optimist's Guide to Thriving in the Age of Accelerations*. Friedman quotes his friend Dov Seidman, who says, "When you press the pause button on a machine, it stops. But when you press the pause button on human beings, they start . . . to reflect, you start to rethink your assumptions, you start to reimagine what is possible and, most importantly, you start to reconnect with your most deeply held beliefs" (2016, 4).

In an age when information is flowing around (and pelting) us constantly, we must teach students the value of slowing down and determining meaning. I realize this ideal isn't easy to accomplish when working within the conveyor-belt-like system of public education, but we must do it. One real research experience per year in each of our classes will add up for our students and will help reinforce their need to become independent learners.

Maryanne Wolf, director of the Center for Reading and Language Research at Tufts University, says that teachers are going to have to help students develop "a bi-literate brain that has the circuitry for 'deep reading' skills and at the same time is adept with technology" (Herold 2014, 24).

If we are to accomplish "bi-literacy," we need to teach students how to read academic material on the Internet. If we show them how to locate and evaluate sources, they might avoid some of the more commercial distractions that appear on most mainstream websites. Students directed to find scholarly articles on high-quality databases are unlikely to encounter advertisements and links to other sites or articles. (For more on evaluating sources, see Chapter 7.)

Herold echoes the Nielsen and Norman findings about people's habits when reading on screens.

> Researchers now say that while many digital texts do a good job of motivating and engaging young people, such texts also pose a number of problems. When reading on screens, for example, people seem to reflexively skim the surface of texts in search of specific information, rather than dive in deeply in order to draw inferences, construct complex arguments, or make connections to their own experiences. Research has also found that students, when reading digitally, tend to discard familiar print-based strategies for boosting comprehension. (2014, 25)

Students do seem to treat text on screens as if it contains little depth. I can only guess why this is so. Perhaps books or articles in print simply look real and solid, whereas text on a screen has a fleeting quality to it. In any case, it is alarming that students abandon sound reading strategies when faced with digital print.

Evidence of the harm done to high school students by using screens for research almost exclusively can be seen most clearly when it comes to higher education. Even the top-performing students in secondary schools find themselves woefully underprepared for the rigors of college work, where they must read and digest large chunks of information independently, take notes in classes, and incorporate that new knowledge (McDaniel 2014). Kathryn N. McDaniel makes this argument eloquently in her essay "Read Long and Prosper: Five Do's and Don'ts for Preparing Students for College." Her number five: "Don't over-emphasize technology for researching, writing, and note-taking. Do give students opportunities to step out of the virtual and into the real world" (2014, 86). Here she emphasizes the fact that the Internet is merely one "path to information" and that "students who understand the many other paths that exist, and know how to use them, will have an edge in higher education and the workplace" (86). McDaniel goes on to say that, although some scholarly sources may be accessible online through databases, it is often better for students to handle manuscripts and other primary sources "in the flesh." She has strong opinions about taking notes in longhand as well. "Beyond the concern that students are checking email or surfing the web while they should be paying attention, professors worry that when students type their notes in class, they become stenographers instead of critically-thinking note-takers who must make choices about what they write down. Also, in contrast to handwriting notes, typing does not seem to help students remember what they have recorded" (86).

Content-area teachers need to increase time spent in class modeling the reading of, and critical thinking about, informational texts unique to their disciplines (disciplinary literacy). English teachers devote a larger chunk of instructional time to reading, modeling, and thinking aloud about literary texts, and they also point out the structural aspects of writing. This practice has served students well; they consistently score higher on reading comprehension of literary texts than on informational ones (Hooley, Tysseling, and Ray 2013, 322).

Dishearteningly, Hooley, Tysseling, and Ray found that there exists a reciprocal cycle of low expectations for student reading: teachers don't expect students to do the assigned reading, and students oblige by not doing the reading. Students are aware of the low expectations because teachers lecture on the texts they assign instead of leading class discussions about them. Students are never asked what they got out of the reading and can count on the teacher explaining it all to them anyway (2013). Our students suffer. A good number of them are unprepared to handle the academic reading they must do in college because we don't expect them to learn from, or hold them accountable for, reading on their own. We have allowed students too many excuses for not doing independent reading. Students (and sometimes parents) prioritize sports, work, and other activities over schoolwork, and we accept it. If academics is to have any integrity in the future, we must insist that students do the work from this day forward. It will not be easy, but it must be done if students are to become thinkers. The powerful elite believe that most people don't read and analyze information. They take advantage of citizens every chance they get. This thought keeps me awake at night.

Crocodiles, alligators, and turtles are among the oldest species on earth. Paleontologists and other scientists theorize that their skeletal and genetic designs are the key to their survival on Earth for millennia, despite climate change and predators. I like to think of basic literacy skills—reading, writing, analyzing, connecting, transferring, extrapolating, and applying—as "crocodile skills." These skills stand the test of time. Regardless of subject matter, medium, or delivery, people will always need to be able to understand communication, analyze and think critically about it, manipulate it, and apply it to their situations. Once students have mastered these crocodile skills, they can use screens—and any other media they encounter in the future—effectively. Literacy skills are the ones that will go the distance, but they must be learned and tested first.

## Analysis: Dealing with Data Sets

In Chapter 2, I briefly mentioned the difference between qualitative and quantitative research. Qualitative research tends to consider more ethereal information (people's feelings or ideas, characteristics, etc.), whereas quantitative research is numbers oriented (the number of times a particular reaction to certain stimuli occurs, temperatures at which matter changes form, etc.). Some perceive qualitative data as more subjective than quantitative, but both are valuable in terms of the creation of knowledge.

Students who have never been called upon to thoroughly analyze, or use, the information they located or compiled will need some guidance and scaffolding initially. Here is where they will fully appreciate the importance of a well-developed research question, claim, or thesis statement. When we analyze data, we are always looking for relevance to, and deviation from, our original ideas about a subject.

The steps in the analysis process are as follows (adapted from University of Leicester n.d.; Pell Institute 2017):

1.  Read carefully through all notations, questions, marks you made on the text(s).

2.  Create categories and subcategories of information and sort your data.

3.  Observe the "story" the data are showing.

4.  Determine whether your findings support other research on the same subject.

5.  Determine whether the data supports or refutes your original ideas.

6.  Decide on your audience—who would benefit most from this knowledge?

Sorting data requires students to establish the main points of their argument, or what they're learning through the study. These need to be somewhat clear, but the data will reveal the "story." Our students need to be able to decipher the implicit information. In other words, they must read between the lines, make correlations, spot patterns, and notice irregularities so they can draw conclusions from their perceptions and what the data show. Let's go back to the Jackie Robinson example. Students can look for others who were the first in their respective fields to break through discriminatory barriers or practices and find commonalities and contrasts.

Coding qualitative data, also called *constant comparative analysis*, has three stages. First, students will need to examine the data to look for common themes. Second, student researchers will determine whether categories exist and, if so, what they are. They will need to label the various categories, sort the data, and code the corresponding information accordingly. We must show our students how to code data. Third, student researchers must go between the data and their theories, validating or refuting them (Gerber et al. 2017). Here I provide an example of data sorting and analysis for the Jackie Robinson research, using a matrix system for organization.

Figure 4.1 is a matrix of notes about the collected data.

| NAME/SEX/RACE | EVENT | YEAR | FACTS SURROUNDING |
|---|---|---|---|
| Wheatley, Phillis Female African American | Published poetry book, London Championed by community of women First to try making a living by writing | 1773 | Had sponsors: her "owners," Countess of Huntington, prominent women in her community of Boston. Published several letters and poems. Had a breakthrough when countess got her book published in London. Slavery in force although she was freed. |
| Walker, Madam C. J. Female African American | Self-made millionaire | 1917 | Developed and sold a line of hair-care products for African American women. Expanded to other beauty products later. Was the illiterate daughter of sharecroppers who were former slaves. No sponsors, but her second husband helped her with marketing and opening a mail-order business. Jim Crow laws in force. |

**Figure 4.1** Notes from biographical data collected

| NAME/SEX/RACE | EVENT | YEAR | FACTS SURROUNDING |
|---|---|---|---|
| Earhart, Amelia<br><br>Female<br><br>White | Flew solo across Atlantic Ocean | 1932 | Was nurse's aide during World War I. Paid for own flying lessons and bought a plane with a loan from her mother. Sold the plane and worked as a social worker. George Palmer Putnam invited her to be the first woman to travel as a passenger on a plane across the Atlantic in 1928, which got her recognition. Putnam sponsored her and her love of flying; they married in 1931. Women not part of workforce. |
| Robinson, Jackie<br><br>Male<br><br>African American | Broke color barrier in MLB<br><br>First-ever Rookie of the Year<br><br>First African American inducted into Baseball Hall of Fame | 1947<br><br>1947<br><br>1962 | Son of sharecroppers. Threw himself into sports. Served as a second lieutenant in World War II at Fort Hood, Texas. Branch Rickey, manager of the Brooklyn Dodgers, wanted him on his team. Sponsored him by encouraging Jackie to endure a rough year on the minor league team. Jim Crow laws in force, but some attitudes in MLB had changed. |
| Sifford, Charles L.<br><br>Male<br><br>African American | PGA golfer<br><br>First African American inducted into Golf Hall of Fame | 1960<br><br>2004 | Learned to play golf working as a caddie at a whites-only country club in North Carolina. He had to leave because he got so good, the members "reacted badly." Moved to Philadelphia, where public golf courses were open to African Americans, but golf was still segregated so he couldn't go pro. He sued the PGA in 1957. He was never allowed to play in the Masters tournament, and he had no sponsors. Jim Crow laws in force. Discriminatory policies and bylaws in PGA. |

**Figure 4.1** Notes from biographical data collected (continued)

| NAME/SEX/RACE | EVENT | YEAR | FACTS SURROUNDING |
|---|---|---|---|
| Bridges, Ruby<br><br>Female<br><br>African American | Integrated white public school in Louisiana | 1960 | Parents put Bridges into the William Frantz Public School in New Orleans. Brown vs. Board of Education ruling in 1954; anti-discrimination legislation followed. No more Jim Crow laws. |
| Stokes, Carl Burton<br><br>Male<br><br>African American | Mayor of Cleveland, Ohio | 1967 | Became a lawyer and then was appointed assistant city prosecutor in Cleveland. Received sponsorship from NAACP, Southern Christian Leadership Conference, and Congress of Racial Equality to help him in his bid to become elected mayor of Cleveland. Anti-discrimination laws in force. |
| Ride, Sally<br><br>Female<br><br>White | Traveled in space | 1983 | Highly educated. Sponsored and encouraged by her parents. Earned PhD in sciences. Applied for opportunity to participate in space program with NASA, which had begun to accept women. Went into space aboard the space shuttle *Challenger*. Later served on the committee investigating the *Challenger* explosion in 1986. Became a sponsor of STEM programs especially for girls. Women fully in workforce. |

**Figure 4.1** Notes from biographical data collected (continued)

As I read through the biographical and factual information about these individuals, the following categories emerge:

- Sex: three male; five female
- Entertainers (sports figures or other)
- Sponsorship
- Race: six African American; two white
- Year of accomplishment
- Prevailing laws/attitudes at the time of accomplishment

When I sort the data according to these categories, it looks like this (Figure 4.2):

| NAME | SEX | RACE | YEAR | SPONSOR | LAWS/ATTITUDES | ENTERTAINER |
|------|-----|------|------|---------|----------------|-------------|
| Wheatley, P. | F | AA | 1773 | "Owners"<br><br>Countess Huntington<br><br>Boston women | Slavery in force | Y |
| Walker, C. J. | F | AA | 1917 | Second husband helped with marketing | Jim Crow laws in force | N |
| Earhart, A. | F | W | 1932 | Mother<br><br>Putnam (spouse) | Women not in workforce or pilots | Y |
| Robinson, J. | M | AA | 1947<br><br>1947<br><br>1962 | Branch Rickey, Dodgers manager | Jim Crow laws in force, but some attitudes changed in MLB | Y |
| Sifford, C. | M | AA | 1960 | None | Jim Crow laws ending<br><br>Discriminatory policies and bylaws in PGA in force | Y |
| Bridges, R. | F | AA | 1960 | Parents | Jim Crow laws ending | N |
| Stokes, C. | M | AA | 1967 | NAACP, SCLC, CORE (political groups) | Anti-discrimination laws in force | N |
| Ride, S. | F | W | 1983 | Parents | Women in workforce<br><br>NASA changed policies toward women | N |

**Figure 4.2** Example of data sorting

Looking at the story the data reveal, I can make the following observations/ conclusions:

1. Half of the people examined in this study were *helped* by changes in prevailing laws and attitudes: Bridges, Ride, Stokes, Robinson.

2. Half of the people examined in this study were successful *in spite of* the prevailing laws and attitudes: Wheatley, Earhart, Sifford, Walker.

3. Society set barriers and individuals broke them.

4. Sponsors may have been a very significant factor. It didn't have to be financial sponsorship—many of the people studied had sponsors who spoke well of them or provided encouragement but didn't provide any financial support.

5. Hard work may have played a more significant role in the success of these individuals than the entertainment factor.

6. Based on when these accomplishments occurred, the United States underwent a significant change in the mid-twentieth century—not only in civil rights equality but also in gender equality.

Notice that I sorted facts according to commonalities that I found in my reading. Students can choose to highlight similarities or differences in many ways. Creating Venn diagrams, plotting graphs, and color coding are just a few ways the coding can be done. We can ask students to show us this work so we can see their thinking and analysis process firsthand and make sure they keep to the focus of their study.

After looking at these data, I can conclude that my theory that the entertainment factor may have been the impetus for some of these breakthroughs may not be accurate. This conclusion is not a failing at all. It's an exciting development! I've learned something from the reading and facts, and I can say a lot about this finding—and all the others—in my presentation. (And *none* of it will be plagiarized!)

I am also left with more questions:

1. How can we measure the impact of sponsors?

2. Is there a causal relationship between civil rights legislation and success for African Americans and women?

3. Is hard work more of a factor than anything else in measuring individual success?

4.  What does the "American dream" mean for people who aren't white? Women?

5.  How much did World War I influence societal change in America?

To answer some of these new questions, I need to look at a larger sample and do some reading about World War I. I am theorizing that it was World War I that prompted change in America because it was the biggest event I can think of that preceded the dates I see in the data. I could find out, after reading about it, that this theory is incorrect as well. Or it could be spot-on. (That's the excitement of research!) These suggestions can be findings of this study too.

As the preceding example shows, analysis requires higher-order thinking. Students can't get to analysis without using data literacy, information literacy, and advanced literacy skills. If research is to be a rich learning experience, students must become skilled in literacy. According to Sam Wineburg, in *Historical Thinking and Other Unnatural Acts: Charting the Future of Teaching the Past,* "Reading is not merely a way to learn new information but becomes a way to engage in new kinds of thinking" (2001, 80).

Analysis of our reading brings us to new kinds of thinking—that is the value of doing it. Thinking is what's missing from "how school works," as the freshman student pointed out on page 31. When all we require of students is to unearth and present raw facts, to define or say "what" something is and nothing more, we curtail their learning. We need to give students ample opportunities to wrestle with informational material until it yields what they need.

## Synthesis

The requirements of the particular study should indicate the format of the presentation. For example, my friend's eighth-grade science students create Rube Goldberg contraptions to display their knowledge of the laws of motion and other principles of physics. The demonstrations last only seconds, or maybe a couple of minutes, but they represent hours of work and show, without a doubt, that her students learned from their questioning, experimentation, and research. Not all the contraptions are successful, and this "failure" is another growth opportunity. The evidence of learning is on display for anyone who cares to look, and her students are proud to describe the process of how they arrived at their designs. (I save the cardboard tubes from paper products all year for this project—you'd be surprised by how many of her students need to make their machines!)

If we wish to give students opportunities to enhance or practice academic writing, then research (term) papers are the traditional way for them to demonstrate their understanding of a subject. Written papers can come in many formats, such as the argument or persuasive essay, rhetorical pieces like editorials, reviews of literature, and reports. In all of these formats, we must encourage students to go beyond the "what," or defining the problem—to move toward analysis and, if warranted, possible solutions to the problem. I am making a plea, once again, to allow real research to be a place where students grapple with their big questions and search for their own truths, even though it may be uncomfortable for us. I agree with Umberto Eco, who says that a teacher's job is to "keep students' minds in shape," "stimulate thinking," and "provoke students to invent ideas" (2015, xxvi).

An excellent way for students to express themselves in writing is by creating a multigenre project. Multigenre projects start with a claim or a research question. Students research the question, gather information, and analyze it. Then, instead of writing a traditional paper, they express their findings through multiple pieces that can take many forms (almost any form, actually), such as poetry/lyrics, epitaphs, letters, journal or diary entries, drawings, and more. The parts of the project are made into a cohesive whole by a repeated phrase or form, called a *repetend*, that threads throughout. These projects are fun for students to write and for us to read. They allow students a lot of choice about how to present their learning and knowledge in multiple genres or formats, and they encourage reflection on the research process. Students submit a letter to the reader explaining the genesis of the idea or question at the heart of their project and how they came to create the pieces they did. The other pieces of the project are constructed with particular attention to form, revolve around the themes of the problem the students studied, and reflect learning in a creative way, encouraging them to transform information.

Another valuable aspect of the multigenre project is that it gets students out of summary mode. There is simply no room for summarizing in an original poem, an epitaph, or any other creative piece. Working in various genres is the ultimate act of synthesis. Tom Romano, who perfected the art of teaching students to create such projects, says, "Genres of narrative thinking require writers to be concrete and precise. They can't just *tell* in abstract language. They can't just be paradigmatic. They must show. They must make their topics palpable. They must penetrate. And that is what multigenre papers enable their authors to do" (2000, 26).

Multigenre projects are not just for English class. Students can, for example, create multipronged public service campaigns to inform their audience about all sorts of social problems using the following formats:

Thirty-second broadcast spots

Letters to the editor or stakeholders

Charts/infographics/graphs/photos

Editorials/rhetorical writing

Scientific journal articles

Short personal narratives

Replicas of historical documents

Written pieces such as these can be used to demonstrate understanding and creation of new knowledge, and to bring attention to real problems in local communities or in the world. By itself, the act of deciding on the appropriate audience for their work is an assessable indicator of students' learning. (See Tom Romano's book *Blending Genre, Altering Style: Writing Multigenre Papers* for more information on guiding your students through creating multigenre projects.)

Students, in my experience, fear having to give oral presentations. They forget that *they* are the presentation and rely on the PowerPoint or Prezi they created to convey information. It is good practice for us to encourage students to present their projects in person. Well-developed speaking skills are valued in employment situations and help students with other literacy skills. In addition, oral presentations allow the entire class to benefit from newly created knowledge and to engage in active listening, which is another important literacy skill. We can teach student audience members to ask pertinent questions of presenters instead of listening passively (or daydreaming). If done well, oral presentations can be engaging for everyone present.

For students who wish to present their learning using digital tools, the possibilities are endless. Students can create blogs, photo essays, video and audio clips, advertisements, web pages—the forms of expression have increased exponentially, as have the audiences for these pieces.

In Chapter 5, I discuss responsible use of information, including copyright issues and citing of sources. These subjects will be especially important for those who create content that is posted to audiences outside of the school building.

# Reflection

Reflection is the most disregarded part of research. Most students are in a time crunch to hand in their work and do not consider reflecting on the efficiency or effectiveness of their research process. Also, we typically don't grade them on reflection, so most will skip it entirely—which is a shame, because reflection can be a valuable learning tool for future research project situations. Scientists finish their studies by reflecting on the process: *What could have gone better? What was done well? What questions remain?* We might consider collecting reflective pieces from students or opening the reflection up to classroom discussion after research. Figure 4.3 includes some student reflections on their research process.

Process Paper (Background History of the Writing) –Adapted from Linda Rief *Read Write Teach*

| Name: | | Date: | 03/27/17 |
|---|---|---|---|

| Title of your piece: | Making a Difference |
|---|---|

**Tell me everything you can about how this writing came to be. Please be as specific as possible in your responses.**

**How did you decide on your photograph that inspired this piece of writing?**

I wasn't here the day we picked our photos. I heard that the photos were about the Civil Rights movement and segregation. I found a picture about school segregation and I wanted to know more about school segregation back then. I chose that picture and then started doing research.

**Where did you find your research sources? Were some sources more helpful than others? Discuss.**

I found my research notes on the historical content site Ms.Beidleman gave us. The sources that benefited the most were the notes on school segregation and the Brown V. Board of Education because it helped me find more information on school segregation as a whole and the Brown V. Board of education helped make school segregation illegal. I took some notes on the Jim Crow Laws, but they weren't as effective as the Brown V. Board of Education and school segregation

**Which note taking method did you use? Discuss your reading/note taking process.**

While I read each of my sources, I would take down notes on the note taking paper Mrs.Fraser gave us while I read each source. I've been doing the method my whole life and it has always been effective.

**Figure 4.3** Students reflect on their research process.

Process Paper (Background History of the Writing) –Adapted from Linda Rief's *Read Write Teach*

| Name: | | Date: | 3-27-17 |
|---|---|---|---|
| Title of your piece: | Dedication | | |

**Tell me everything you can about how this writing came to be. Please be as specific as possible in your responses.**

How did you decide on your photograph that inspired this piece of writing?

I chose this photograph because I knew I would be able to incorporate some prior knowledge I had on a girl named Ruby Bridges into this story. The picture showed protesting in front of a school, and from this, I was able to elaborate and show what I knew!

Where did you find your research sources? Were some sources more helpful than others? Discuss.

I found one of my sources on the database and this was all about Ruby. This was very helpful because I was able to learn more about her family, her, and the accomplishments she had in her life. The second source I had I found online and this source was not as helpful, but still helpful. This sight talked about other important people which I chose not to incorporate into the story because I didn't want it to become confusing with different characters.

Which note taking method did you use? Discuss your reading/note taking process.

I chose the note taking method of using the nline graphic organizers. I chose to go this route because it was already an organized sheet and I know that I am not the most organized student so I didnt want to risk hand writing them and then losing them.

---

Process Paper (Background History of the Writing) –Adapted from Linda Rief's *Read Write Teach*

| Name: | | Date: | 3-27-17 |
|---|---|---|---|
| Title of your piece: | The Year of Change for the United States and Me | | |

**Tell me everything you can about how this writing came to be. Please be as specific as possible in your responses.**

How did you decide on your photograph that inspired this piece of writing?

I liked the photo with the two girls the most. It just spoke to me, but then everyone else picked it. This wasn't all that bad though because I had more time to actually scroll through all of the pictures. I ended up picking the last one. FDR is just such an amazing man and the picture really spoke to me.

Where did you find your research sources? Were some sources more helpful than others? Discuss.

My book source was so helpful. From just a half a page of that book I learned so much about FDR and his life. I found this book in our school library. My first source was from the database that you gave us. It gave some helpful foundation knowledge that I didn't exactly use facts from in my piece, but more of the mindset of that time period. One of the sources I used the most was a site that had FDR's whole speech on it. This was very helpful to hear his tone instead of the tone I wanted to give him. I also used pieces of the actual speech in my journal entries to show the comparison.

Which note taking method did you use? Discuss your reading/note taking process.

I used the comparison notes. I liked the ability to have the space to right down my reaction. I had to think more about the facts or other things I took down. This helped me internalize it, which in turn made my piece more authentic and less about shoving facts in.

**Figure 4.3** Students reflect on their research process. (continued)

# A Word About Comfort Zones

In well-written fiction, conflict is introduced almost immediately. I am aware that what I'm saying in this book may bring conflict to you, the reader. A step-by-step guide on how to get students to do this stuff—all the rigorous parts of scholarship involved in the research process—would be nice to have. Many of us haven't done research ourselves in years or even decades, so how are we supposed to assign it and then assess it? It's just easier for everyone involved to continue doing what we're doing. We have standards that our administration enumerates and monitors, and then tallies the instances when we meet them (or don't) in our instruction. Our students are at different ability levels—how can we get all of them to perform proficiently with literacy and research skills? And then there is time. If we allot the time students need to accomplish research as I am describing, will we see an immediate return on that investment? A future return, even?

First, all people process things differently because they come to reading with their own prior knowledge formed by everything they've ever encountered in their environment. Their questions and ideas are as unique as they are. In the absence of a step-by-step guide, I hope what I have proposed here shows us all the steps to research and makes us think about how our students approach this work.

Second, I have no magic solution to the time or standards issues. Those of us in education, on any level, work against the clock every day. We are asked to hit ever-changing standards a certain number of times every term while being constrained by the length of the period/block, the length of the school day, the days of the week, the weeks in the term, and the contracted days in the year. Then we have the mandatory school assemblies and other activities in which students must participate if they are to be well-rounded that take place outside of school hours but encroach upon our class time nonetheless.

Perhaps the biggest, most daunting conflict I'm presenting here is the suggestion that we must let go of the controls for a time and allow our students to drive the bus. We must let them experience independent learning when everything within us screams, "Danger, Will Robinson!!!" Students themselves are reluctant to leave their comfort zones— passivity is often easier for them and for us.

The trouble is, we *know* the status quo needs to be thwacked.

Students need to be challenged to do more than seek simple answers to surface-level questions. The life we are helping prepare them for isn't going to give them a free pass.

Research is a learning process in two ways: the action of carrying it out and the discoveries students make. As with any process, research operates on a continuum, which means you might be present to witness students' "aha" moments, but more often than not you won't. I tell students all the time that the bulk of their learning from doing research will most likely occur outside the hours of class time. So, the answer to the question *Will I see an immediate return on the time investment?* is a big, definite *Maybe*.

What I can tell you with absolute confidence is that, despite our wariness of ceding control, our uncertainty, and the huge chunks of time our students need to allow their thoughts to coalesce, research done right is definitely worth doing.

# Chapter 5

## The Importance of Documentation

*The true test of a man's character is what he does when no one is watching.*

—John Wooden

A note to readers: This chapter is about citations and proper use of intellectual property. Because this book is a work of academic writing, I am beholden to the rules of academia and so have used sources in the manner appropriate for this work. The style and format of citations and sources in this book (including this chapter) are Chicago—specifically, Chicago's author-date style—as required by the publisher. However, for purposes of discussion and example in this chapter, I demonstrate and model Modern Language Association (MLA) style citations. The rules for these citation styles differ, and I don't want to muddy the waters by discussing both. I have worked hard to be clear about citations and proper use of intellectual property, which are very important concepts (but confusing to *everyone*) in the process of research. Some excellent guides that can be used as resources are listed later in this chapter. I hope this information is useful.

## On Plagiarism

After much inner debate, I decided not to give plagiarism its own chapter. Students know what it is: turning in someone else's work as your own. I firmly believe most students want to avoid plagiarizing. Of course, there will always be a percentage of students who try to cut corners because they leave their work until the night before it's due, and copying a paragraph of text from a source and pasting it into their own document fills up half a page. (Let's face it, nothing good happens after midnight . . .)

The problem here is really twofold. First, our assignments can set up students for plagiarism. Say, for example, that a science teacher has just taught a unit on the water cycle. As part of the unit, students receive notes and information on the water cycle, including graphics. The teacher then assigns a report on the water cycle and asks that students include a graphic that shows the different stages. If that is the entire assignment and the teacher doesn't mention that citations are required, a student may simply turn in the graphic that was included as part of the unit information as his or her own work. The resulting report is a work of plagiarism. For topic-based assignments such as this, we should instead ask our students to say something about our content and their understanding of it.

Let's return for a moment to my sixth-grade biography report assignment. Yes, it was great that I was held accountable for the reading, but a book report—repeating facts from the biography—requires low-level skills. Turning these types of assignments into higher-order thinking exercises would make them a much richer experience for our students and us. Instead of asking for only a summary (which is inarguably a good skill for students to demonstrate), we could also request that students compare or contrast the famous person's life with their own. The assignment could read like this:

*Choose a biography of a famous American. Read the book and write a paper that includes the following:*

A brief summary of his or her life

How was his or her life similar to the way we live now?

How was it different?

How does the time period in which he or she lived affect these similarities and/ or differences?

How would you describe what kind of person he or she is? How do you know?

*Please be sure to use specific examples and evidence directly from the text to support your claims. Please include the page numbers on which you found the evidence and a bibliography at the end of your paper.*

In order to meet the requirements of this assignment, students may have to access some additional information from sources outside the original text, thereby extending their reading and expanding their knowledge.

The water cycle assignment could be framed in this way:

*Describe the water cycle and explain how your understanding of it applies to your daily life. Be sure to include a hand-drawn illustration and source citations.*

The second factor that largely contributes to student plagiarism is lack of practice in expressing their own ideas about their learning. Most of the time we are checking for content (understandably), and we don't give students any real opportunities to analyze or synthesize the information. Students are bewildered when suddenly an assignment requires gathering information from multiple sources.

If we expect and require students to say something about every fact, quote, summary, or paraphrase they use in their writing, the lines that divide their thoughts from others' will become much clearer. Students need to practice saying something about their evidence as often as possible, even in speech.

In other words, students need to react to their nonfiction reading instead of simply zeroing in on "answers." We ask them to analyze character, setting, theme, and story in literature—why not ask them to look at informative pieces of writing with an analytical eye as well?

Developing students' note-taking skills will help them see where an author's thoughts end and theirs begin, and making this line more distinct will cut down on incidents of plagiarism. (For more on note-taking, see Chapter 4.) Double-entry journals can be used to practice this skill as well.

# Citing Sources

Most people are utterly confused about when and how to cite sources in their finished presentations. This aspect of properly using information has always been a challenge, but now, with all the various formats and locations in which information can be found, it is even more complicated. First, students need a consistent message about *when* to cite sources. (I discuss *how* to cite sources in detail later in this chapter.) Sources must always be acknowledged with both in-text* and full citations when

- information is summarized from a text, a transcript, or an interview;

- information is paraphrased from a text, a transcript, or an interview;

- information is directly quoted from a text, a transcript, or an interview;

- discipline-specific phrases, language, statistics, or vocabulary are taken directly from a text, a transcript, or an interview; or

- charts, graphs, maps, photos, schematics, diagrams, links, poems, art, videos, music, or cartoons are copied directly into a research project. (Permission from the creator or author of any of these may need to be obtained before they're used. See page 115 for more information.)

*In-text citations are parenthetical references that are made in the body of a text. Often, they are marked by the author's last name, a page number, and, depending on the format of the citation, sometimes a year of publication. Using Chicago style, they look like this: (Fraser 2018, 3). The in-text citation provides a brief summary of the source, pointing the reader to the complete source information included in the text's bibliography or references section.

The first two items in the preceding list often give high school teachers and students pause. Students are taught how to summarize and put text into their "own words" (i.e., paraphrase) in elementary school, and that this approach is "good enough" when using information. Although summarizing and paraphrasing are great skills to have, they are lower level in terms of critical thinking. The habit of changing words around but not identifying whose ideas they are can muddy the waters when students grow older and are required to distinguish their own thinking from that of their sources. This causes big problems when the bottom line is quite simple: if the student didn't know it before reading about it, *it must be cited.* Period. No exceptions.

Elementary teachers would do students a great service if they taught them to delineate information gathered from a source and their own thinking; this could be accomplished by requiring students to say something about every quote, summary, fact, and paraphrase. For example, a modified double-entry journal might look like this:

| Fact in Your Own Words | Say Something |
|---|---|
| Tree frogs are green and yellow so they can hide from predators but they have other colors too. | It is a good thing they are the same colors as leaves so animals won't be able to eat them. |
| Brown bears hibernate all winter in caves or hollows. | How do they eat when they sleep so long? They must be very skinny when they wake up in the spring. |
| Goldilocks ate all of Baby Bear's porridge. | Should Goldilocks have gone to jail? |

Most elementary-age students already understand that taking something that doesn't belong to you is wrong. (Academic dishonesty is the central theme of the book *Junie B., First Grader: Cheater Pants*, by Barbara Park.)

In college, or at work, it is never "good enough" to paraphrase or quote authors or creators without giving credit to them or asking for and obtaining permission to use their ideas or creations. Politicians, speakers, and musicians have been called out on this error in public—one recent example saw Conan O'Brien's team of writers taken to trial over a claim of joke theft (Gardner 2017). At best, it causes them embarrassment and loss of credibility. At worst, it costs them millions of dollars, plus embarrassment and loss of credibility. All this pain could be easily avoided.

One way to ensure that students focus on their own ideas in their writing or presentation is to allow them to conduct primary, action, or original research on a controlled basis. As I said in Chapter 3, students need to understand the nature of their inquiry and embark on research with sources that complement that inquiry. If the questions originate from the students themselves, and they are asked to hypothesize, gather data, read, annotate, and analyze those data against the original inquiry and then communicate their findings in a synthetic form, the number of incidents of blatant and brazen plagiarism will fall dramatically. It is simply impossible to plagiarize analysis of one's own data set.

As an example, I worked with a student who was involved in a problem-based learning project in which he identified a problem and devised a possible solution using existing or created technology. It greatly bothered him that students frequently leave their trash on tables in the cafeteria instead of throwing it away after lunch. First, we discussed the issue. I wanted him to understand that what he was looking at fell within the behavioral science field, but I didn't want to explicitly identify this for him because he needed to make the connection himself. To help him along, I reminded him of the story I told during Freshman Seminar about my dog, Iggy (see pages 58–60). I told the student that I saw some similarities among Iggy's behavior, my behavior, and his current questions about student behavior. I let that sit for a couple of minutes and then asked, "What are you considering for possible solutions to the trash problem?"

"I'd like to set up an automatic text that would be sent to each student's phone in the last five minutes of the lunch period as a reminder to clean up their area," he responded.

This thinking is sound. Students can use their phones during lunch, and everyone responds to texts. So I asked, "How will you know if that text is changing students' behavior?"

"I guess I can look around at how much trash is left."

Next, I asked, "How could you get some baseline information to see how much of a problem the trash really is?"

He had to think about that question. This student was a sophomore, and he didn't have experience with data collection or the knowledge and vocabulary of behavioral science, but he was onto something here. My colleague, his teacher, reminded me about the seat-belt law and how newer-model vehicles now come with a light that reminds the driver to buckle up *and* a timed—and *annoying*—audible alert that chimes at specific intervals until compliance with the seat-belt law is attained. This is a prime example of a technological solution that induces specific behavior, or behavior modification.

How can our students learn the terms and details of subjects about which they know little but that are relevant to their chosen study? The same way I learned about the various meanings of the word *sterling* (see page 38): they need to read about the subject(s) and derive meaning, at their developmental level, from texts. They need to talk to people in the know. They need to be able to see where they have gaps in their knowledge and pursue learning opportunities.

## Why Cite?

In my experience as an educator, I have given and seen many, many assignments. Invariably, the ones that call for research include an exhortation to use MLA formatting for citations. And yet, I'm not sure whether students are given any consistent instruction on how to create in-text and full citations. With great gusto, I give our freshmen lessons on citing sources, but it is not enough. My lessons consist of informing students about why they must cite sources, as I have done here, but it is impossible to go over how to cite every kind of material. That lecture would take days or even weeks and be totally boring and probably cause students' eyes to glaze over. Instead I tell them what information goes into every citation: name/corporate sponsor, title, publisher, and year or date published. I demonstrate how to make in-text (parenthetical) citations by writing a quick paragraph on the board and inserting a quote that I make up, as in the following example. (Note the signal phrase, "According to Garp." When there is a signal phrase, the author's name already appears in the quote so just the page number goes in the in-text citation.)

*According to Garp, the world is "a wild and wonderful place" (p. 62). Garp is, of course, delusional when he makes this statement, but he illustrates here the concept of perception versus reality.*

We know that students often learn best through repetition, so they would benefit from seeing us model citing sources multiple times in many classes. We can do this by pursuing an inquiry in front of the class and then acknowledging the source by creating a full citation on the screen or board for our students to see. We might struggle a bit with this task. We may have to use a reference to look up how to cite a particular type of material. Allowing our students to see us grapple with creating proper citations is beneficial. They will see that the rules of academia apply to everyone, and that these rules may not always be comfortable. It is all right to struggle with them at first.

Putting this idea into practice, let's imagine the following scenario:

*Students are listening to a lesson in biology on mammals' origins, and one of the students asks about how mammals evolved. Going to the Internet, the teacher puts in the search term* mammal evolution, *which returns more than 70 million hits, the first several of which are from Wikipedia, of course. Showing students that she is selective about sources, the teacher scrolls down to a wonderful article from* National Geographic *titled "The Rise of Mammals." The teacher points out that* National Geographic *is an authoritative source (and that the library subscribes to the print magazine, so the school community has access to the digital archives [shameless library marketing]), so she clicks on the link and logs in. As a class, they read the information in the article that answers the question. Satisfied, the students then have a brief, impromptu discussion about how the article relates to the content of the day's lesson. The teacher says she'd like to save the article to refer to later and suggests writing a citation. The class works on it together and creates this MLA-style citation (note the hanging indent):*

Gore, Rick. "The Rise of Mammals." *National Geographic*, 14 Feb. 2018,
    www.nationalgeographic.com/science/prehistoric-world/rise-mammals/.

The other problem students face with citations is that they have difficulty identifying where the material they consulted originated if it was something other than a book. For example, did they read an interview online? Take an excerpt from a broadcast or a blog? Did the information come from a multivolume work? No guide in the world will help if our students don't know how to classify the information they used. In Chapter 3, I provide a chart that shows some of the various information types that can be used based on the nature of the inquiry. Deciding where to look for information *before the start of research* (another plug for having a plan) can help students eliminate the bewilderment of creating citations at the end.

Explaining why we have to cite sources is an important way to help students understand the evolution behind the process. The reasons for citing sources are twofold. First, acknowledging the sources from which information is taken protects intellectual property and copyright. Authors and organizations that have conducted thorough studies and then generated research papers, books, or other material have a considerable investment in this information that can include incurred expenses and, certainly, time. Authors and corporate sponsors deserve credit for doing the work and formulating the ideas that went into the presentation, paper, book, blog, and so forth.

Second, academic work requires that we separate our ideas from those of others. It must be clear to the reader what the newly created knowledge is, and what or who inspired it. In-text citations and the Works Cited or bibliography section alert the reader to the separation of ideas and knowledge and allow him to refer to the same sources if he so chooses. According to the *MLA Handbook*, "Plagiarists are seen not only as dishonest but also as incompetent, incapable of doing research and expressing original thoughts" (2016, 7). We want our students to competently express their original ideas and questions.

Giving credit to creators, artists, musicians, and so forth is also required under copyright law. People often confuse copyright and citation. I attempt to clarify the two in the next section.

# Copyright Vs. Citation

Copyright and citation overlap in a lot of places. As mentioned previously, use of material that someone else created must be cited in academic work, because citing shows respect to, as well as acknowledgment of, the person(s) whose idea(s) you are referencing in your own work. On the other hand, copyright laws protect creators from loss of credit and, ultimately, money.

There are important distinctions between copyright and citation. All work that is cited is protected by copyright. Anyone who publishes work of any kind is covered under copyright (unless he or she deliberately chooses not to be), which means that to legally use the material as part of another creation, a consumer must obtain permission from the creator. These protections exist to prevent theft of intellectual property. Think about it. Artists, authors, lyricists, and other creators earn their living producing creative works. Using their work without permission is the same as stealing apples from the supermarket. Consumers are just as liable for taking an idea as they are for taking a tangible object.

Some exceptions to copyright laws exist, which I will explain. I want to make the point that awareness of copyright and following the rules is now a much larger, and more complicated, concern during this time of exploding technological advances. We are encouraging students to bring their work to larger audiences, outside of school—which is terrific!—but this comes with the responsibility to be good stewards of created material. It is incumbent on all of us to make our students aware of the restrictions and exceptions of using existing published material and to ensure that they work within legal parameters. We need to set a good example and comply with the laws ourselves.

Student work often extends far beyond the classroom walls these days, and so it should. We encourage students to use myriad formats: podcasts, photo essays, blogs, and on and on. Our students share their work via many channels: online, before the public, and in Google Classroom. Although Google Classroom is closed to the public, information can be copied and shared elsewhere, and we must be aware of this fact.

When student work or your handout lessons remain within the confines of your classroom, there are exceptions to the copyright laws. Most of us have heard of "fair use" exemptions, but do we follow these guidelines and instruct our students on them? We spend a lot of time speaking of and reminding our students about properly citing sources, but we don't spend much time teaching students how to use sources, artwork, or other created material in their work.

There are four guidelines we must follow to be in compliance with fair use exemptions under copyright law. The first is "purpose and character of the use"; this guideline "looks at how those copying the work are going to use it" (Butler 2011, 13). You can make copies of an article to use for a classroom lesson, but you may not sell that article. Others' work can also be used "for purposes such as criticism [or] comment" (US Copyright Law, as cited in Butler 2011, 14). Under this guideline, it is allowable to transform a creative piece of work or to quote from it. You cannot, however, take a logo—for example—and use it unaltered in another creative piece without permission.

Guideline number two is "nature of the work" (Butler 2011, 14). This exemption allows for use of published nonfiction work in a research paper or lesson. In other words, this guideline is intended to instruct us in the use of material for our own research projects. We may use published nonfiction work (i.e., research studies, articles, informational texts) in our own writing with proper citation; however, using a piece of creative fiction, as yet unpublished, may not be allowable. Always consider what kind of material you are using when including it in academic work.

The third guideline under fair use speaks to the amount we are borrowing. Our aim should be to use the smallest amount of the work possible. We must consider the length of the whole piece versus "the amount needed to achieve the objective of the copying" (Butler 2011, 14). We must also consider how substantial the part we want to copy, or use, is relative to the whole piece. If we copy the "heart of the work," even if that is just thirty seconds of it, it may be too much (14). (Remember, these guidelines apply to students' use of material too.) We must be careful not to show a whole movie if we can get our point across using just a ten-minute clip.

The fourth fair use guideline pertains to the "marketability of the work" (Butler 2011, 14–15). Put simply, if what we do causes the creator/owner/author to lose money, we have violated copyright law. An example is photocopying consumables such as workbooks. If we buy one book and photocopy the pages every day to make class sets, we are causing the publisher to lose money. Each workbook is intended for use by one student, and new ones should be purchased in bulk every year (if we must continue to use them). Another example that Butler mentions is copying scripts for a play (2011). Script publishers have licensing agreements because plays are proprietary. An author or corporation receives royalties for every copy of the script that is rented and for live performances (which people are restricted from recording or photographing). Once play troupes enter into the licensing agreement, they are entrusted to behave legally with the licensed material. The same principle applies to public performances of movies, hence the warnings posted at the beginning of every movie on DVD or Blu-ray. Schools can pay for a public performance site license, which allows for the legal screening of movies in the building for educational and even recreational purposes. An annual site license will cost around a few hundred dollars; the cost is determined by school population size.

If you have questions about copyright, please consult your school librarian or IT director. If neither of those roles exists at your school, I recommend obtaining a department or school copy of *Copyright for Teachers and Librarians in the 21st Century* by Rebecca P. Butler for reference. You can also consult the US Government Copyright Office online at https://www.copyright.gov/fair-use/more-info.html. This site addresses every question imaginable, contains case studies, and is the ultimate authoritative source on copyright.

Most college and university libraries have information on their websites about fair use guidelines and copyright. One thorough and comprehensive site is Oviatt Library at California State University, Northridge: http://libguides.csun.edu/copyright/basics. This site contains an easy-to-use infographic and other helpful material that can help you determine whether you and your students are following copyright laws.

## Creative Commons

Creative Commons (https://creativecommons.org) offers all sorts of works free of, or with limited, copyright restrictions. Students can find all kinds of digital artwork, photos, freeware, music, papers, videos, research, and cultural works that can be used. Each work has a list of the restrictions imposed, such as attribution (e.g., giving credit to the creator, a link to the license, and making note of any changes made to the work). These rules tell users how the work can be used and what credit needs to be given.

The rest of this chapter will center on citation, but please do keep copyright compliance in mind. It is increasingly important that students understand their responsibility toward the law and intellectual property as digital citizens, especially when they enter the workplace.

## Distinguishing Between Paraphrasing, Quoting, and Summarizing

In an earlier chapter, I mentioned that it takes some real practice to write academic papers that smoothly incorporate information from sources. Notice that I didn't say *seamlessly* incorporate. Academic work requires a visible demarcation of ideas—

specifically, whose ideas are whose. We must make sure students understand that even though access to information is free and easy, they are *not* free to consume it without acknowledging the source. There are three ways researchers include information from sources in academic papers, presentations, speeches, videos, visual displays, and so on: direct quote or quotation, paraphrase, and summary.

In most student papers I've seen at the secondary level, students provide parenthetical citations (in-text citations) only for direct (word-for-word) quotes taken from sources. Sometimes these quotes don't make sense in the piece because they're not relevant to the point being discussed. Students simply find catchy sentences they like and paste them into the paper—probably because the assignment required a certain number of quotes. Instead of using the information organically to provide necessary evidence, clarify a point, or bolster or refute an argument, the use of source material is perfunctory and results in contrived student work. The worst part is that students remain in the dark about why they have to use sources in the first place.

In Figure 5.1, I share a lesson I created to help students think about how they're using source material in their academic writing, and to emphasize the point that they need to cite the sources they summarize and paraphrase as well as quote directly.

For this lesson, I read aloud a passage from Chris Crutcher's excellent novel *Deadline* (2007). I explain that as readers, we bring our knowledge and experience to any reading we do. I read the passage—in which a high school senior, who wants to hear his diagnosis alone because he's eighteen years old, learns that he has terminal cancer. From my perspective as a parent with older children, I tell students that as I read the passage, I began to think about what it means when a kid turns eighteen and what it means to be an adult, and how one day on the calendar can have such a major effect. Then I wonder aloud if kids are ready for these changes and effects, and I conclude that most people aren't ready at age eighteen to take up the mantle of adulthood and that the age of majority should be increased to twenty-one. Next I give them an essay I wrote with that thesis statement, in which I've left three blank spots for supporting information from Crutcher's text.

I tell students that they will have to go along with my argument even though they probably disagree with it because their perspective is totally different from mine. The Freshman Seminar teachers and I have students work in pairs to complete this exercise. When students are done, I ask them to provide an explanation for which format they chose (quote, summary, or paraphrase) and the purpose for using that format to convey their information. A few of the students' responses to this exercise are included as examples.

Names: _____ Teacher: _____ Period: _____

For each exercise read the left-hand column (mark up the text if needed) and follow the directions in the right-hand column. Use the passage on the right for the one on the left.

In the text below, please underline the thesis statement.

Fill in the blanks with text or ideas from the passage on the opposite side of this page that support the thesis statement, whether you agree with it or not. Decide whether you should use summary, paraphrasing, or direct quotes.

Please look up any words you don't know or can't guess the meaning of from context. Be sure to include proper in-text citations. Add extra pages if you need more room.

## An Argument for Making Twenty-One the Age of Majority in the United States

For most teenagers, turning eighteen is a big deal. It means they can vote, serve their country in the military, leave high school, make decisions without consulting their parents, and legally buy lottery tickets. That one day on the calendar is certainly a huge occasion, but there is some question about whether eighteen-year-old people are ready and able to make serious decisions that could impact the rest of their lives. Pushing the age of majority up to twenty-one makes quite a bit of sense.

Often kids turning eighteen occurs while they are still in high school which means that most likely they are still dependent on their parents for basic needs – shelter, food, clothing, etc. In addition, their education is incomplete, and their experience limited. Parents have made the decisions, major and minor, for their whole lives up until that point.

But one day on the calendar changes all that. Or does it?

In the book, *Deadline*, Chris Crutcher tackles this question with his main character, Ben Wolf. **(citation 1)**

_____

_____

_____

_____

Healthcare is a major concern for most people. People may actually choose certain jobs or companies to work for based on health insurance benefits. Most

---

Excerpt from *Deadline*, by Chris Crutcher (pp 2-3).

Doc Wagner left a phone message a few days after my routine cross-country physical; he wanted to see me with my parents in his office either ASAP or pronto. There was *gravity* in his voice, so I decided I'd better scout ahead to see if his message was PG-13 and suited for all, or R-rated just for me. Turned out to be the X.

"Hey, Ben," he said as he passed me in the waiting room. "Where are your folks?"

"They couldn't make it."

"I'd really prefer they were here."

"My mom's... well, you know my mom; and Dad's on the truck."

"I'm afraid I have to insist," he said.

"I'll relay the information. Promise."

He said it again. "I'm afraid I *have* to insist."

"Insist all you want, my good man," I said back. "I'm eighteen, an adult in the eyes of the election board and the Selective Service and your people, the American Medical Association. I decide who gets the goods on yours truly." Dr. Wagner has known my family since before I was born and was plenty used to my smart-ass attitude. He's delivered probably 80 percent of the town's population my age and under, including my brother, and I'm not even close to his worst work. He also delivered Sooner Cowans.

"I don't feel right talking about this without your parents, Ben," he said, walking me toward the examination room. "But I guess you leave me no choice."

"I leave you exactly that," I said. "Lay it on me."

And lay it on me he did, and I am no longer quite so glib.

| Summary: | condensing a long passage into its main idea(s) in a few sentences |
| Paraphrase: | putting ideas from a text into your own words |
| Direct Quote: | taking sentences or text directly out of a passage and putting them into your own work without changing them |

**Figure 5.1** Source material lesson

eighteen-year-olds do not have full-time jobs and are therefore ineligible to carry their own health insurance. In fact, the Affordable Care Act allows for children to stay on their parents' health insurance until the age of twenty-six. Since parents are paying the bills, they should be clued in on what is happening with their children's health. Ben Wolf doesn't think so. **(citation 2)** _____

One has to wonder whether Ben is emotionally ready to hear Dr. Wagner's news.

At twenty-one years old, most people have completed their high school education, and possibly college too. The level of maturity and experience are also better developed at twenty-one. Despite his "smart-ass attitude", there is evidence that Ben Wolf might have regretted his decision to hear the doctor's diagnosis alone at eighteen years old. **(citation 3)** _____

While some might argue that twenty-one is also a very young age for people to make important, life-changing decisions on their own, it is clear that for most people a lot of development takes place after the age of eighteen. It is time society recognized this idea by making twenty-one the legal age of majority.

---

In the box below, please circle the type of citation you selected and explain why you used that information to fill in the blanks in the essay above. For example: does it explain? Is it evidence? Does it make a point clearer?

Citation 1:     Summary     Paraphrase     Direct Quote

Purpose for using this material in the piece: _____

Citation 2:     Summary     Paraphrase     Direct Quote

Purpose for using this material in the piece: _____

Citation 3:     Summary     Paraphrase     Direct Quote

Purpose for using this material in the piece: _____

Please write a full citation for the source provided: _____

**Figure 5.1** Source material lesson (continued)

Names: __Izzy & Juliahna__    Teacher: __Troendle__    Period: __1__

For each exercise read the left-hand column (mark up the text if needed) and follow the directions in the right-hand column. Use the passage on the right for the one on the left.

In the text below, please underline the thesis statement.
Fill in the blanks with text or ideas from the passage on the opposite side of this page that support the thesis statement, whether you agree with it or not. Decide whether you should use summary, paraphrasing, or direct quotes.

Please look up any words you don't know or can't guess the meaning of from context. Be sure to include proper in-text citations. Add extra pages if you need more room.

### An Argument for Making Twenty-One the Age of Majority in the United States

For most teenagers, turning eighteen is a big deal. It means they can vote, serve their country in the military, leave high school, make decisions without consulting their parents, and legally buy lottery tickets. That one day on the calendar is certainly a huge occasion, but there is some question about whether eighteen-year-old people are ready and able to make serious decisions that could impact the rest of their lives. Pushing the age of majority up to twenty-one makes quite a bit of sense.

Often kids turning eighteen occurs while they are still in high school which means that most likely they are still dependent on their parents for basic needs – shelter, food, clothing, etc. In addition, their education is incomplete, and their experience limited. Parents have made the decisions, major and minor, for their whole lives up until that point.

But one day on the calendar changes all that. Or does it?

In the book, *Deadline*, Chris Crutcher tackles this question with his main character, Ben Wolf. **(citation 1)** In the book Ben Wolf learns that he has been diagnosed with cancer. Ben decides that he isn't going to tell anyone including his parents, and since he's 18 he doesn't have to (2-3)

Healthcare is a major concern for most people. People may actually choose certain jobs or companies to work for based on health insurance benefits. Most

---

Excerpt from *Deadline*, by Chris Crutcher (pp 2-3).

Doc Wagner left a phone message a few days after my routine cross-country physical: he wanted to see me with my parents in his office either ASAP or pronto. There was *gravity* in his voice, so I decided I'd better scout ahead to see if his message was PG-13 and suited for all, or R-rated just for me. Turned out to be X.

"Hey, Ben," he said as he passed me in the waiting room. "Where are your folks?"

"They couldn't make it."

"I'd really prefer they were here."

"My mom's... well, you know my mom; and Dad's on the truck."

"I'm afraid I have to insist," he said.

"I'll relay the information. Promise."

He said it again. "I'm afraid I *have* to insist."

"Insist all you want, my good man," I said back. "I'm eighteen, an adult in the eyes of the election board and the Selective Service and your people, the American Medical Association. I decide who gets the goods on yours truly." Dr. Wagner has known my family since before I was born and was plenty used to my smart-ass attitude. He's delivered probably 80 percent of the town's population my age and under, including my brother, and I'm not even close to his worst work. He also delivered Sooner Cowans.

"I don't feel right talking about this without your parents, Ben," he said, walking me toward the examination room. "But I guess you leave me no choice."

"I leave you exactly that," I said. "Lay it on me."

And lay it on me he did, and I am no longer quite so glib.

| | |
|---|---|
| **Summary:** | condensing a long passage into its main idea(s) in a few sentences |
| **Paraphrase:** | putting ideas from a text into your own words |
| **Direct Quote:** | taking sentences or text directly out of a passage and putting them into your own work without changing them |

**Figure 5.2** Student responses to the source material lesson

eighteen-year-olds do not have full-time jobs and are therefore ineligible to carry their own health insurance. In fact, the Affordable Care Act allows for children to stay on their parents' health insurance until the age of twenty-six. Since parents are paying the bills, they should be clued in on what is happening with their children's health. Ben Wolf doesn't think so. **(citation 2)** _I'm afraid I have to insist." "I'll relay the information." "Promise"_ This is an example of Ben telling his doctor he doesn't want his parents to know. (Crutcher, 2-3)

One has to wonder whether Ben is emotionally ready to hear Dr. Wagner's news.

At twenty-one years old, most people have completed their high school education, and possibly college too. The level of maturity and experience are also better developed at twenty-one. Despite his "smart-ass attitude", there is evidence that Ben Wolf might have regretted his decision to hear the doctor's diagnosis alone at eighteen years old. **(citation 3)** _And lay it on me he did." and "When Ben says this he is glib"_ showing us that maybe he wasn't prepared to hear his news without his parents (Crutcher, 2-3)

While some might argue that twenty-one is also a very young age for people to make important, life-changing decisions on their own, it is clear that for most people a lot of development takes place after the age of eighteen. It is time society recognized this idea by making twenty-one the legal age of majority.

---

In the box below, please circle the type of citation you selected and explain why you used that information to fill in the blanks in the essay above. For example: does it explain? Is it evidence? Does it make a point clearer?

Citation 1:  (Summary)  Paraphrase  Direct Quote

Purpose for using this material in the piece: _We used a summary to summarize the book and help support the thesis statement._

Citation 2:  Summary  Paraphrase  (Direct Quote)

Purpose for using this material in the piece: _The quote shows Ben convincing the doctor not to have his parents there_

Citation 3:  Summary  Paraphrase  (Direct Quote)

Purpose for using this material in the piece: _This quote is an example of Ben showing his glib discussion on the news without his parents_

Please write a full citation for the source provided: _Crutcher, Chris. "Deadline." Hoper Collins Publishers 2007_

**Figure 5.2** Student responses to the source material lesson (continued)

Most secondary students are skilled at summarizing. In fact, summary makes up the bulk of secondary students' papers—what is missing is the attribution or citation. Summarizing is similar to retelling. It shows us that the student made some meaning of a text and can recall it in the correct sequence. Summary is useful in academic work, especially when students are writing reviews of literature, but summaries should never stand alone. Analysis of the piece that shows the reader why the information supports or refutes a thesis or claim should immediately follow (or may even precede) the summarized material. An in-text citation should always appear at the end of the summary passage, and a full citation should be included in a bibliography or Works Cited.

Direct quotation is exactly what it sounds like: using the author's exact words (and punctuation) in academic writing. Direct quotations are offset by quotation marks if they are approximately four lines long or less. Any quotes more than four lines long must appear in a block, indented and single-spaced with no quotation marks. (There are several examples of both block and shorter quotes throughout this book.) All direct quotations must be cited in-text at the end of the quoted material and have a full citation in the bibliography or Works Cited.

Direct quotes should be used sparingly and only when they are so well-written and apt that the student couldn't say it any better himself. I have seen assignments that require students to use a certain number of direct quotes—for example, one per paragraph. I recommend not quantifying the number of quotes students need in an academic paper; this could encourage plagiarism by forcing students to create contrived situations for quotes or to pad a Works Cited with sources they didn't use except to quote them to meet a requirement. This requirement may also cause writing to suffer because the student must break the flow of her own ideas to artificially insert another's. Use of quotes in writing should be authentic, organic, and up to the author. And, as with summary, an analysis of the quote should follow—in other words, no stand-alone quotes. Students need practice inserting quotes from sources into their work, but requiring a quote in each paragraph is not the best way to accomplish this. Please remember the tremendous power we wield with our assignments. If we require it, students (mostly) will comply.

Paraphrasing involves putting pieces of a text into one's own words in lieu of a direct quote. This technique is the least disruptive in terms of writing and reading because it does not halt the flow of ideas in the piece. It might be difficult to get a fifth grader to understand the concepts of attributions, intellectual property, and academic honesty, but at the middle school and secondary levels, we must ensure students' understanding of these ideas and practices. Our students need to adhere to the rules of academe when they embark on academic work. They are not too young to understand that ideas that are not their own need to be attributed by citations to the person or people to whom they belong, *even if the students have reworded them*. Analysis of the paraphrased information should be embedded in the writing as well—again, no stand-alone paraphrased material.

The put-it-in-your-own-words habit is hard to break. It's baked into our students' writing process, and—let's face it—it's easier for us to let it slide.

But we can't.

We need to adjust our view of students, from vessels into which we decant knowledge of our discipline to creators of knowledge. As consumers and creators, our charges join a vast and distinguished body who all follow guiding principles when working with questions and information. According to the *MLA Handbook*,

> Academic writing is at its root a *conversation* [emphasis mine] among scholars about a topic or question. Scholars write for their peers, communicating the results of their research through books, journal articles, and other forms of published work. In the course of a project, they seek out relevant publications to learn from and build on earlier research. Through their own published work, they incorporate, modify, respond to, and refute previous publications . . . Students are called on to learn document styles, in a range of courses throughout their education, but not because it is expected that all students will take up such research practices in their professional lives. Rather, learning the conventions of a form of writing—those of the research essay, for instance—prepares the student to write not just in that form but in others as well. (2016, 5)

Working in an academic form is part of the educational continuum for all students. Just as there are codes of ethics for police and other professionals, some exist for academics as well.

Requiring and assessing research notes may help move students toward better research and writing practices. I am also a huge fan of the annotated bibliography. If we require students to speak about how they used their sources, they will think about how that information fits into their own ideas or preconceived notions. Figure 5.3 is an excellent example of a student's annotated bibliography as part of a multigenre project. (This student's complete project appears in Appendix C.)

Annotated Bibliography

When a President Says "I'll Kill You". Dir. Andrew Glazer and Jeremy Rocklin. New York
Times . New York Times, n.d. Web. 11 Apr. 2017.

This Source was the one that truly got my project started. I found it while scrolling
through the New York Times website and the title really interested me, "When a
President Says 'I'll Kill You'." It was a video including the president of the philippines
giving a brute speech to a room of professionals telling how anyone involved with drugs
should be rid of *HIS* country- killed off. It showed graphic images of people who have
been claimed by this effort of his war on drugs. Their loved ones were showed crying
hysterically above them, being pushed away by the police. "Why are you here, Lito? You
were just alive!" One of the girls screamed this and it sped my heart rate. I had found
something worth writing about. It was a journalistic and expository video to show what
was going on in the philippines. It gave me a lot of inspiration as well as helpful
information for my research. It showed me what was happening in this other part of the
world and how that could affect so many people.

Stanton, Gregory H. "Ten Stages of Genocide." Genocide Education Project . The Genocide
Education Project, n.d. Web. 11 Apr. 2017.

I got this source from my world history class a month or two ago. We were learning about
genocides around the world like the Holocaust and the Rwandan genocide. The article is
basically a formula for how a society can engage in genocide. It goes through the ten
stages that have shown to be common themes in all genocides and dissects and
explains what they mean and how it happens. When I was doing my research about
what was happening In the Philippines, I started to recognize some of the signs and
themes of a genocide. I looked more into this article after that and it gave me lots of
useful information to help guide my writing. It helped me make accurate points about my
topic with a source to back up my statements and observations.

Iyengar, Rishi, et al. "The Killing Season inside Philippine President Rodrigo Duterte's War on
Drugs." Time , vol. 188, no. 14, 10 Oct. 2016, pp. 46-49. EBSCO host,
search.ebscohost.com/login.aspx?direct=true&db=aph&AN=118457516&site=ehost-live.

I found this source kind of in the middle of my research and It seemed like just what I was
looking for. It discussed what was going on in the Philippines from a journalistic point of
view. It went into details of arguments from both points of view using quotes and such.
This gave a political perspective but most likely in a bias way, they pulled quotes from
speeches Duterte had given as well as some from people who support him. It showed
how a lot of Filipinos support his actions and think that what he is doing is right and truly
the best option. It also gave many statistics that I think really helped me in digging into

**Figure 5.3** A student's annotated bibliography

this topic further and kept me wanting to learn more. It also made me realize that a lot of others saw this as a problem, but no one yet had even begun to compare it to a genocide and that's what made me really want to write this. It is a piece to put it out there that this is what I think and how i'm perceiving it, even if it doesn't leave the english classroom.

---

Santos, Ana P. "A Philippine Senator Defies Her President - from behind Bars." Los Angeles Times , Los Angeles Times, www.latimes.com/world/asia/la-fg-philippines-delima-20170326-story.html. Accessed 25 May 2017.

My last two sources are very similar to my third in the sense that all three are journalistic pieces. All go over the same topic and have pretty much the same argument, but each of them added something original and new to my piece. This article starts showing the reader what kind of person President Duterte is. It gives an example of a local senator that called for an investigation into his bloody drug "solution". He responded with many forms of violence from verbal threats to make her cry to promises to throw her and jail and destroy her. After such an introduction the piece explains further what the recently elected leader had been doing and how it is affecting individuals lives in the Philippines. This article really helped me to get that perspective and build on my pieces that include voices from individuals like that.

Jenkins, Nash. "Death Reigns on the Streets of Duterte's Philippines." Time , vol. 189, no. 3, 16 Jan. 2017, pp. 28-37. EBSCO host , search.ebscohost.com/login.aspx?direct=true&db=aph&AN=120565248&site=ehost-live.

This is one of my most recent sources. It focuses on the conditions of the Philippines as of 2017. It is almost the same thing as "The Killing season" but this source has the newest updates on things like death tolls and how the government is continuing to function in the country. This is also one of my shorter sources but It still had a lot to offer and contributed to my piece. It also talks about life in the slums of the Philippines, where drugs seem to be a bigger issue. It helped me form my voice not only for a victim of this situation but also a supporter. All of these people are coming from the same places under very similar conditions but have such varying views on this conflict. This article helped my understand that more fully and helped me to try and recreate the variety.

**Figure 5.3** A student's annotated bibliography (continued)

We can see that this student read, understood, and reacted to all of the sources she used for this project. Her ideas are very clear and distinct from those of the authors. Also note the high-quality, authoritative sources she consulted.

## Intellectual Freedom = Part of Literacy

When using information or art, researchers are called upon to safeguard intellectual freedom. The fact that researchers use and incorporate the work of others when developing their own ideas and work obligates them to act ethically throughout the process. It constitutes a tacit agreement; if we participate in the creation of the collective knowledge of mankind, we honor and keep the trust bestowed by those who have gone before us and that will be shown to us in the future. Information is ubiquitous. It can be found everywhere in our environment. We must never forget that every piece of information was created and placed in public by a human being and, as such, represents that human being. We are not free to simply take it as our own. Not now. Not ever.

Jole Seroff considers information access a value. We take for granted that information is available and accessible to us 24/7:

> Intellectual freedom is not a value we hold in a vacuum but, instead, in a particular time and place. Throughout history and across the world today, unfettered access to information is the exception not the norm. It is our responsibility to exercise and defend this freedom in our own society, while striving to understand the historical and political contexts that frame this issue differently in many cultures around the world. (2015, 24)

Seroff also presents the idea that citation or "attribution" is "not just a chore"; it allows students "to participate in creation and sharing of knowledge" (2015, 23). We must prepare our students to take their place among the academics. This responsibility applies to all students, even those for whom a high school diploma may mark the end point of formal education.

## Instruction on Citation

Many of us left college quite a while ago and may have only vague memories of how to cite sources ourselves, so I want to provide specific examples of different citations for this chapter. This is, however, a tall order. There are so many different kinds of material.

First, and most significant, citation instruction is an excellent reason to enlist the help of the school librarian or media specialist. He or she can provide actual instruction on citing sources, but there are a couple of provisos: (1) Please, *please*, ask for the librarian's help before the start of a project, and (2) allow him or her the time to meet and work with students *all the way through*. Information literacy skills are best learned and absorbed if students can see how they apply to the project at hand. Students have no chance of retaining these skills if they are taught in isolation. Partnering with the librarian for the duration of a project is a lot more effective than a stand-alone lesson on citations or a one-time lesson on available resources in the library that has no connection to an ongoing project.

In the absence of a librarian, some excellent and helpful guides provide specific examples of how to cite all types of materials. I highly recommend *A Pocket Style Manual*, 7th ed. (make sure it's the one that includes the MLA 8 update) by Diana Hacker and Nancy Sommers (2015). This handy, spiral-bound book lists the manuscript and citation formats for Modern Language Association (MLA), American Psychological Association (APA), and Chicago styles. It is the most practical and comprehensive guide available, in my opinion.

Certain disciplines require specific style formats (and here's where it gets confusing):

- Humanities studies use MLA style.
- Social sciences studies use APA style.
- Historians (and sometimes humanities studies) use Chicago style.

We teach MLA style to our students because most of their research occurs in humanities courses. Your school may have adopted one of the other styles. Sticking with one citation style makes it easier for secondary students to practice academic rules of writing and research.

According to Hacker and Sommers, all full citations in MLA style contain an "author, creator or producer," title, and date of publication (2015, 133). Our students need to record this minimal information every time they consult a source. This information represents only the skeleton and should by no means be accepted as a full citation. We can even provide generic examples of citations for sources that may be used most commonly.

If we are frustrated by a lack of examples, then we now have a clear understanding of how our students feel when we assign these projects with no examples for them and then penalize them for plagiarizing. Get a good manual and learn along with your students. For every source I used in this book, I had to consult my style manual (in this case, Chicago). I needed to know what type of material I was using and to be able to cite my sources properly (e.g., book, article [from a journal/database/online], interview). I am in serious trouble if I fail at this task in a published book. Citing sources is part of the requirement for communicating academically and needs to be practiced over and over again. Review my bibliography at the end of this book. Check out reference lists at the end of other professional readings and research studies. Follow some in-text citations to the bibliography or reference list to see the full citation.

Most important, model this work for students. Remember what Donald Graves said: if we assign it, we must do the work ourselves.

### *Modern Language Association Generic Examples of Full Citations*

(to be placed on a Works Cited page or bibliography at the end of a research paper or project) for most commonly used source formats.

**Book with one author:**

Last name, First name. Title (in italics). Publisher, Year. Hanging indent if the citation goes two or more lines.

Butler, Rebecca P. *Copyright for Teachers and Librarians in the 21st Century*. Neal-Schuman, 2011.

**Article online:**

Last name, First name. Title of Article (in quotation marks), Title of Website (in italics), Date published, URL.

Gardner, Eriq. "Judge Rules News Publishers Violated Copyright by Embedding Tweets of Tom Brady Photo." *The Hollywood Reporter*, 15 Feb. 2018, https://www.hollywoodreporter.com/thr-esq/judge-rules-new-publishers-violated-copyright-by-embedding-tweets-tom-brady-photo-1085342.

Every kind of source has its own format for full citations. Please see the *MLA Handbook*, 8th edition, for more information on how to cite all source materials in MLA format.

More than half of the trouble our students run into with citations stems from their evaluation of sources. If they are not consulting authoritative sources, they will have a hard time generating a full citation in any style. Authoritative sources are not just the rigorous, peer-reviewed articles found in books or on academic databases. A blog entry written by Tony Hawk about skateboarding or Ozzy Osbourne on the rock music industry is an authoritative source. (Just totally dated myself here . . .) All authoritative sources will have an author or a corporate sponsor, a title, and a publication date, at a minimum. The authors and creators are out there for all to see. (More on authority and evaluating sources in Chapter 7.)

## Public Domain and Common Knowledge

Information that is considered in the public domain or common knowledge does not have to be cited. *Public domain* refers to material that is not protected by copyright because the creator chooses to share it without restriction with the public, material for which copyright protection has expired or wasn't renewed, or material that the law does not protect. Generally, all government publications are in the public domain because they are produced using public funds. If a work is not in the public domain, it must be cited in academic settings or pieces and permission must be obtained from the creator before the work can be used for public performance or in publications.

The rules regarding public domain are a bit complicated because of the evolution of copyright law. Generally, public domain items include the following:

- Most federal documents (there are some exceptions)
- Phone books
- Works with expired copyrights
- Works for which creators or owners have chosen to give up their copyrights
- Freeware
- Some open-source documents
- Works registered with Creative Commons and similar organizations
- Things that cannot be copyrighted—for example, names, short phrases, titles, ideas, and facts
- Some clip art (Internet and print)
- Works published in 1923 or before
- Some works published between 1923 and 1963 (Gasaway 2003)

Another wrinkle with citing sources is the concept of *common knowledge*. According to the *Academic Integrity at MIT* handbook, common knowledge is "information that the average educated reader would accept as reliable without having to look it up" (Massachusetts Institute of Technology n.d.). Common knowledge is "information (or facts) that most people know" (e.g., water freezes at 32 degrees Fahrenheit); "knowledge shared by members of a certain field" (e.g., the laws of physics); "information shared by a cultural or national group" (e.g., historic figures or events). "However, what may be common knowledge in one culture, nation, academic discipline or peer group may *not* be common knowledge in another" (Massachusetts Institute of Technology n.d.).

Things that are considered common knowledge do not have to be cited. An application of this idea in our classes: a book, an article, or an essay that the whole class has read doesn't have to be cited in a class assignment that requires evidence from that particular book, article, or essay. (Example: Class reads *Fahrenheit 451*. Assignment is to describe in an essay how the dystopia genre can be prophetic using *Fahrenheit 451* as one example of a dystopia.)

Sometimes what is considered common knowledge is subjective. "The best advice is: When in doubt, cite your source" (Massachusetts Institute of Technology n.d.).

## Citation Generators: Yes or No?

My sister is a pharmacist. When she was in school at the University of Rhode Island, she learned how to make pills and tablets. She was required to purchase a pill mold and was taught how to grind up the compounds for various medications and press them by hand into the molds. Over the course of her thirty-plus-year career as a pharmacist, she has never actually had to make her own pills, but she understands exactly what the process is and what goes into medications.

Even if your students will not need to cite sources in their everyday lives once they are out of school, they will benefit from knowing how to do so. Thus, I encourage caution when using citation-generating sites. These websites provide some easy-to-follow examples of citations. However, I remain unimpressed with the citation-generating abilities.

Students must use a somewhat inflexible digital form. Because a student only needs to fill in a form to generate a citation, he doesn't have to understand what he's doing. This lack of understanding is evident in the glaring errors that occur when fields in the form are left blank. Citation generators will fill in these empty fields with something—usually n.d. (no date) or n.p. (no page). Students' lack of knowledge shows when they don't fix these incorrect citations created by citation generators before pasting them into a Works Cited page. I have rarely seen a generated citation come out error-free. If students are going to use these—and I know they will—they will have to check that every single citation is formatted correctly and includes the author's name, the title of the work being cited, the publication date, the name of the publisher, proper punctuation, and so on. (Personally, I don't understand how it's easier for students to use citation generators when they have to check everything they spit out, but they *will* insist on using them.)

In Freshman Seminar, we teach our students to create citations by hand using an MLA guide as a reference. By creating all of their citations from scratch, students learn the patterns of citations for all types of material and how each one differs from others; they also can see what goes into a full citation (much like my sister making the compounds for pills from scratch). They must get somewhat intimate with the sources and understand the finer points of citing. This also helps with source evaluation because if there isn't enough information on the source to create a proper citation, it probably isn't a good source to use. Using a citation generator robs students of this valuable learning opportunity.

# Chapter 6

## Assessment

*The way I see it, if you want the rainbow, you gotta put up with the rain.*

—Dolly Parton

## Assignment Design Is Crucial

When I was a junior in high school, I participated in an interdisciplinary course called American Studies. This opportunity was an honors-level course composed of English 11 and American History classes that met separately. There were twelve of us in the course, and it was interdisciplinary to the extent that the text we read in the English class corresponded with the time period we were studying in the history class. I do not recall any other overt attempts by the teachers at putting any of the readings into a context in history, or vice versa. What I do recall vividly is the research paper.

As a culminating project we were assigned a term paper, which was considered a rite of passage among students at our high school. The paper carried as much weight as each quarter grade, meaning it was worth 20 percent of the final grade in both the English and history classes. It was to be a long paper—at least twenty pages typed—and we had to procure a copy of Kate Turabian's style manual to use as a resource for citations. (Turabian follows Chicago style; see Chapter 5.)

We were given a dense, four-page list of topics to choose from for our paper. I chose "Taft and the Republican Party Split." I had no idea what I was doing, except that I knew the paper had to be at least twenty pages, I had to consult sources, and citations were required.

In the "old school" way, we wrote our research on 3-by-5-inch index cards along with corresponding citations. We had an individual meeting with the teachers to discuss how the research was going. At no point during the process did I feel that I was going astray. My paper ended up being more than thirty pages long; I am sure it was supernaturally boring to read and most likely a rehash of history—unfortunately, the wrong history. As it turned out, I concentrated most of my "findings" on the Sherman Antitrust Act, which was in fact a part of the rift that developed in the Republican Party in the early twentieth century, but it was far from the whole issue. My paper had no central thesis or question to provide focus for the study. I now understand that there was much more that contributed to the destructive chasm in the Republican Party in 1912 than the fact that Taft's interpretation of, and philosophy about, the Sherman Antitrust Act differed from Theodore Roosevelt's. There was also a juicy and prolonged controversy between two men, Richard A. Ballinger and Gifford Pinchot, who were both posturing and playing politics. My paper could have taken many interesting, possibly even groundbreaking, directions.

But it didn't.

I received a D-minus on that paper. A D-minus told me that except for the fact that I'd cranked out more than thirty pages (of what?!), I had failed the project miserably. In short, I learned how not to conduct research. All these decades later, I am still bewildered by the experience.

## What's the Purpose?

In recent years, there has been a movement in education known as Understanding by Design (UbD; Wiggins and McTighe 2005). The basic premise of this philosophy is that educators should decide on outcomes before designing instruction. In implementation, a UbD unit begins with assessments and works backward to ensure that instruction modules support learning so that desired outcomes may be achieved. Every assignment should lead students toward specified understandings derived from curriculum. It's a good practice.

Using UdB, we might consider the purpose of the research assignment and the desired outcomes. Are we looking for students to demonstrate literacy skills in reading, writing, speaking, or listening? Are we looking for our students to go into depth on a particular subject or topic? Are we seeking evidence of problem-solving ability? Are we hoping to improve students' questioning skills? Each of these outcomes requires a specially styled assessment tool. Rubrics are the most common, but we must take care to craft them so that they are tied closely to our specified learning objectives. At the end, our students should be able to see and understand what they did well and where they need improvement. Further, it is very important that we establish the purpose of the research project *before* we assign it so that students are clear about the learning goals and we can design an assessment tool that measures what we are trying to accomplish.

Projects are terrific. They give us real insight into who our students are as learners. There are so many layers and facets to projects. They provide rich opportunities for our students to show us what they learned through the research process, but only if we look for that information. We squander an important opportunity if we only check to see that citations are properly formatted or that spelling and grammar are perfect. Mechanics may be the easiest to assess, but do they show us what we need to see in terms of learning?

Students seem to regard the surface-level aspects of research as very important, often valuing product over process. Our students see what we are showing them: that proper mechanics (citations, grammar, and format) often form the basis of how we assess their work. They are very concerned about finding "the answer," even though this is contrary to real research findings, which usually spawn more questions and point to the need for further study.

Higher-order thinking skills are what we should be assessing in research projects, because that is where students demonstrate their learning. It all comes down to what we hope students will accomplish with the assignment. Are we ranking mechanics on par with, or maybe higher than, original ideas in our students' work?

Often, students' first questions when given a research assignment are as follows:

How many pages does this paper have to be?

How many sources do we need?

Do you want MLA formatting?

When is it due?

This line of questioning is more appropriate for ordering a deli sandwich. Students make papers to order. If they comply with all of the stipulations we set, we are happy and subsequently so are they, adding another good grade to their collection. But why should we settle for this?

### Ten Reasons to Assign Research

Seriously, why do we assign research projects? The results are often less exciting than we hoped, and they take up a lot of time. What are our students even getting out of research projects? Here are ten things:

1. Discerning quality by evaluating information based on reliability, appropriateness, authority, accuracy, and relevance

2. Reading widely on a subject

3. Considering opposing viewpoints

4. Pursuing inquiry—their own, or one suggested

5. Connecting new information to prior knowledge

6. Locating and accessing information independently

7. Hypothesizing/drawing conclusions

8. Internalizing information

9. Transforming information; creating something new—ideas, points of discourse, solutions to problems

10. Reflecting on their learning process

By doing research projects, our students are developing the advanced literacy skills needed to be citizens in a democratic society.

During 2016 and 2017, I partnered with professors from the University of New Hampshire to conduct a study in which we surveyed twelfth-grade, honors-level, college-bound students; college freshmen; and college upperclassmen. We wanted to know what literacy skills (particularly writing skills) transferred from high school to college. Because all disciplines require research writing in some capacity, we centered our study on this area. Our findings apply to assessment, so I will share some of them here.

We asked students whether they value research and how much time they spent on various research tasks, such as deciding on a research question, taking notes/reading the information, and thinking about their work. We also asked students how they went about locating information (Fraser, Lasley, and Williams 2016; Lasley, Fraser, and Williams n.d.).

As I had with my informal survey of sophomores, we found that almost two-thirds of the responses indicated a lack of joy (or full-on dread) at the mere mention of a research assignment. Despite the dread, nearly three-quarters of the students said that research is important to them, yet 63 percent of high school students reported spending little time (three hours or less) thinking about their research outside of school, 58 percent reported spending three hours or less reading and taking notes on information they locate, and 58 percent said they spend three hours or less writing the paper or creating the presentation (Fraser, Lasley, and Williams 2016; Lasley, Fraser, and Williams n.d.).

On all levels, students indicated feelings of tension or stress that focused on getting research "right," as in page-length requirements, sources, citations, and so forth. We also found repeated incidents of what we called "blatant teacher talk," which occurred most often in response to our question about choosing sources. Forty-four percent of the students we surveyed used language that seemed to come straight from lessons they received on evaluating sources, such as using sites with URLs ending in .gov, .org, or .edu (Fraser, Lasley, and Williams 2016; Lasley, Fraser, and Williams n.d.). This finding lends credence to my earlier thoughts about giving students a set of criteria by which to evaluate sources. Students do indeed cling to our instruction on evaluating sources as they would a lifeline. In fact, besides the dread, "teacher talk" was the only other aspect our survey showed that transfers from the high school to the college research process (Fraser, Lasley, and Williams 2016; Lasley, Fraser, and Williams n.d.).

# Transforming Information

When we read our students' papers, we should see evidence of transformation of the information they located. The revised Bloom's Taxonomy indicates that students should demonstrate ability in a range of cognitive skills:

**Remember** – Retrieving relevant knowledge from long-term memory

**Recognizing; Recalling**

**Understand** – Determining the meaning of instructional messages, including oral, written, and graphic communication

**Interpreting; Exemplifying, Classifying; Summarizing; Inferring; Comparing; Explaining**

**Apply** – Carrying out or using a procedure in a given situation

**Executing; Implementing**

**Analyze** – Breaking material into its constituent parts and detecting how the parts relate to one another and to an overall structure or purpose

**Differentiating; Organizing; Attributing**

**Evaluate** – Making judgments based on criteria and standards

**Checking; Critiquing**

**Create** – Putting elements together to form a novel, coherent whole or make an original product

**Generating; Planning; Producing** (Krathwohl 2002, 215)

Research is a great place for students to display their thinking. Are we seeing the big idea(s) behind the topic words? Where has the student taken the study? How did the student connect the newly acquired information to his prior knowledge? What was discovered as a result of the study? Is there any sign of the student's voice in the writing? Did the piece succeed as a persuasive essay? Were there any new understandings? Surprises?

If we value higher-order thinking skills, then we need to give more weight to them in the assessment tool. I am suggesting a significant shift in the way we think about student research projects at the high school level. Although it's messy, student research should be about pursuing inquiry, not taking orders. Yes, students are at sometimes vastly different ability levels, but in high school they can be introduced to the higher-order thinking and advanced literacy that real inquiry demands.

## Stimulating Student Curiosity

Many times, students have difficulty coming up with research topics on their own. Quite a few of them prefer to stick with popular standby topics such as abortion, legalizing marijuana, or gun control. Please understand, I'm not trivializing any of these topics—they are all important for us to parse in American society—but in my experience, students perceive them to be well-covered and easy to research. I worry that students who select these topics will descend into writing reports because there is so much information readily available on them. What meaty questions could students come to about them? Most students will simply take a side and use other people's arguments in their paper or presentation.

What I look for are the more organic and immediate concerns of students, such as recent death of a family member because of cancer, a grandparent suffering with dementia (see Figures 6.1 and 6.2), a volunteer experience at a soup kitchen, themes from Poetry Out Loud recitations, and so forth. How do I get there? I interview students. Personal experience is powerful. It's the place everyone starts with making meaning. Students who have participated in life have questions, often heavy-duty ones like *Why does God make good people suffer?* or *How do people become homeless?* There's no search engine in the world that can churn out easy answers to those questions!

Another way to spark students' curiosity is to draw from themes in readings, preferably fiction. We can find fiction stories for any discipline (science fiction, historical fiction, psychological fiction, dystopias), stories about all sorts of social issues (poverty, coming-of-age, abusive families, immigration, racial discrimination/oppression, civil rights, pollution, sexual identity), and so much more. Start a project by having students read fiction to gain a vicarious personal experience or at least develop some empathy for characters in situations unlike their own.

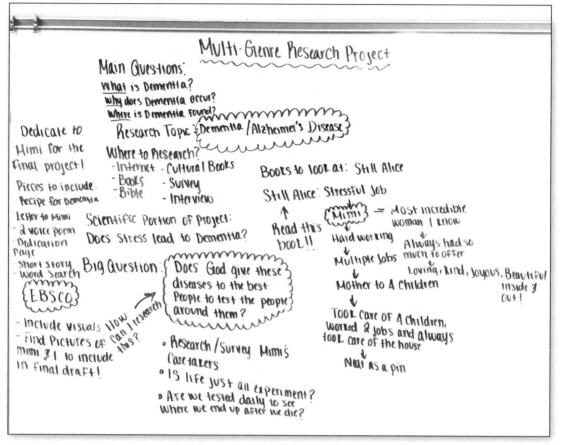

**Figure 6.1** Student mind map: coming to a question

## Monitoring Progress

If we are going to embrace research as a way for our students to gain depth of knowledge and discover something they don't already know, then we must adopt a clear approach to how we monitor the process. The final paper should not be the first one we see from each student. If we use the formative and summative assessment model, we can collect and assess parts of the project along the way. We should check in with students at specified times during the research process so that we can monitor progress, mitigate procrastination, and ensure that our students receive support and encouragement as they work through the process. Coaches give feedback to players during practices and then reflect and review after games. What I'm suggesting is similar to that format. Here's how it could look:

| **Thursday February 15th** |
|---|
| Source (citation): Alz. "Alzheimer's Disease & Dementia." *Alzheimer's Association*, Alzheimer's Association, www.alz.org/alzheimers_disease_what_is_alzheimers.asp. |
| Significant Quote: Alzheimer's is the sixth leading cause of death in the United States. |
| **100+ word quickwrite Research Journal entry - _consider addressing the following questions:_**<br>• What did you learn from reading this source today?<br>• What is your reaction to your reading today?<br>• What perspective does the author of this source present in regards to your research question(s)?<br>• Why is this quote significant?<br>• What does this quote mean in relation to your research question(s)?<br>• What does this quote make you think about?<br>• What further questions has reading this source raised for you?<br>• What new potential search terms (phrases, names, terms, etc.) has this source given you? |
| I never have once thought that Alzheimer's was a key role in the deaths of the United States. I can't believe that Alzheimer's kills this many people. I don't understand how a disease can go from forgetting what you need to buy at the grocery store to forgetting how to eat/drink. I am now terrified to see my grandmother in just a couple of years. Since I have been reading the book, *Still Alice* I have seen what a person with Alzheimer's goes through every day. It breaks my heart that my Mimi is going through this. This definitely brings a lot of concern to my Mimi. I don't know what I am going to do when she doesn't remember me. That is truly my number one fear and I know that it is bound to happen. |

**Figure 6.2** The same student's analysis and thinking after reading about the subject

### *Formative Strategies*

Meet/conference with students as they are working on deciding what to study. Look at notes, mind maps, questions, etc.

1. Require an annotated bibliography or a review of literature to see what sources students are reading and how their questions and ideas are developing.

2. Require notes, double-entry journals, or organizers to see what information students are gathering, whether they've evaluated it, and how they plan to use it to support their thinking.

3. Ask students to show you how they're organizing their thinking, so you can see the progression of their thoughts (e.g., outlines, bulleted list, mind maps).

4. Use individual or peer conferencing to ask questions about process and progress.

5. Preview draft documents, prewriting, and/or quick-writes.

### Summative/Finished Piece Ideas

| | | |
|---|---|---|
| Experiment | Prezi | Term/Formal/Essay Paper |
| Physical Item Created | PowerPoint | TED Talk–style Presentation |
| Podcast | Video | |
| Solution to a Problem in the Community | | Multigenre Project |
| | | Analysis of Data Set |

Remember, the final piece will not be the first time you see the display of students' synthesis.

## Workshop-Style Conferencing with Students

Student conferences are student (or writer) driven. The student speaks first. They can be done one-on-one between you and each student, which takes time but will give you an excellent idea of where each writer stands. While you're meeting with students, others can be working on their writing. Appointments with students can be set at fifteen-minute (or less) intervals and spread out over a couple of days so class time remains for mini-lessons or content. Here are some prompts or questions to ask in a one-on-one conference:

- Tell me about your project.
- Explain your process so far. What have you struggled with? What has gone well? What are your preliminary findings?
- Are the sources you've chosen helpful? May I see your notes (or other information gathered)? (Offer some guidance on notes and sources if needed.)
- Are you feeling confident about your work?
- Do you need help from me or the librarian?
- What are your ideas about how you will organize your final piece?

If time is a concern, you can have students work together in groups to do peer conferencing. In peer conferencing, students prepare a brief, informal presentation about their research project in which they describe their process, the big questions or ideas they're pursuing, and how things are going to small groups of fellow students. (You can have them use some or all of the preceding questions if they need guidance.) The idea is to foster a sense of pride and ownership among students. It doesn't hurt to give our students opportunities to practice their speaking and active listening skills either.

Sometimes students need to pan their camera out a little. A sophomore in an honors English class at my school decided to study the crime of poaching elephants for their tusks. He was having a hard time finding information on this exceedingly focused subject, so I suggested that he look at other precious resources humans are callously depleting and draw some parallels to the elephants. He visibly brightened at that suggestion. When I last spoke with him, he had decided to look at other endangered species and the impact of humans on them. He got "unstuck," which might not have happened if his English teacher and I hadn't conferenced with him during his research process.

Realizing that others are facing the same hurdles can be empowering for our students. They can share how they overcome setbacks or seek advice from their groups. When peer conferencing is taking place, we can circulate around the room and listen in. We can also collect peer review sheets and learn from them. We can do both individual and peer conferencing at specified times during the research process.

What if students won't participate or share their work? Motivation is always a concern, and I have no magic solution. What I *can* say is that our chances of meeting with resistance are reduced if we establish a classroom culture in which our students are encouraged to pursue their own inquiry and study, and we model this academic behavior for our students frequently. The young man interested in a Veterans Day assembly mentioned on page 41 serves as an example here. He sought out teachers and administrators, shared his work, and conferenced with us *on his own time* in pursuit of his inquiry.

## Responding to Student Work

Feedback is huge. Whatever kind of response we have to our students' work makes a lasting impact. When giving feedback to our students, there are a few things we should keep in mind.

***Respect Students as Creators of Knowledge.*** Read student work as we would any of our professional texts. Show them our questions. Show students how we make sense or meaning of a text. Monitor our reading of student work for understanding. Be willing to listen. Annotate.

***Assess the Skills, Appreciate the Ideas.*** Our feedback and comments should be directed at observing skills such as the writing (or other delivery), synthesis, analysis, reasoning, application, and understanding. We should not be looking exclusively for content, conclusions, or philosophies. The most useful evaluation centers on the students' journey.

***Mechanics Should Be Weighted Lightly.*** Try to refrain from placing too much emphasis on grammar, spelling, and punctuation errors. Yes, it is important that students present their work in the best manner possible—it indicates pride in what they've done and it shows respect for the reader or audience. What I am talking about here is using mechanical errors to mask our own worry about not feeling qualified to respond to students' writing. We know a well-expressed argument when we see one.

***The Grade Itself Is Feedback.*** Our feedback should be a tool that students can use to improve. As Alan Alda writes in his wonderful book *If I Understood You, Would I Have This Look on My Face? My Adventures in the Art and Science of Relating and Communicating,* we need to give students "a model of success to live up to" rather than "a vision of failure they somehow have to avoid" (2017, 69). My D-minus was feedback that stuck with me for decades as a glaring failure. Absent was advice on how to fix my mistakes in the future—I received those lessons subsequently, from other educators in my life.

Our assessments should be designed to look for signs of success rather than confirmation of failure. One of the reasons educators detest and resent standardized tests is that they confirm failure. No one wants to be judged on how well they fail. Like my D-minus showed me, those test scores give us nothing but a number. The game becomes about raising the score, and we cannot inform our instruction based on scores alone. Sometimes the pressure to perform causes us to put aside good practice and what we know is right so we can raise the score. Educators hate this. Why would we do the same thing to our students?

Kelly Gallagher cites Douglas Reeves, who calls it "sucker-punch grading" (Gallagher 2006, 148). Keeping students from feedback until the final grade does indeed deliver a "sucker punch," because they have no choice but to accept the number or letter grade and will not learn from it at all. This idea highlights the difference between assessment *of* learning and assessment *for* learning (Reeves 2010, 58). Our feedback should "assess [students'] level of competence," and it should also "help them grow and learn" (58).

Rubrics must be clearly tied to our objectives for the assignment. They also need to show our students what they can do to improve performance. For example, if one of the objectives of an assignment is to address big ideas or questions, the rubric should express that in a way that students can easily understand:

|  | Exceeds | Meets | Developing | Not Evident |
|---|---|---|---|---|
| Piece addresses and identifies big ideas or questions | Piece uncovers groundbreaking ideas and new questions on the topic; completely original | Piece identifies big ideas and/ or questions and leads toward a unique approach to the idea or question | Piece is a report with some mention of a big idea behind the topic | Piece is a simple report of facts with no big ideas or questions |

We want to encourage our students to exceed our objectives and expectations every time on every gradient.

## On Feedback

When we want to improve our ability to respond to student work (their writing, in particular), we need look no further than Peter Elbow and Pat Belanoff, who wrote a wonderful book called *Sharing and Responding*. In this book, the authors explain the purpose of writing and provide frameworks for responding to all sorts of writing. Their explanation can give us more clarity on why we assign research projects in the first place. "Because all school writing is evaluated, we sometimes assume that the *point* of writing is to be evaluated. When we speak to people, do we immediately ask them how *good* our words were? No. We speak because we are trying to *communicate*. We certainly don't expect listeners to give us a grade. With sharing we're trying to emphasize writing as communicating rather than as performing for judgment" (Elbow and Belanoff 1989, 9).

Elbow and Belanoff describe several structures for responding to writing, but I will mention only two of them here because these apply to writing in any discipline: "IIC. Descriptive Responding" (18) and "IIIA. Analytic Responding: Skeleton Feedback" (27). (Hereafter I refer to these as just "descriptive responding" and "analytic responding.")

Elbow and Belanoff suggest these criteria for descriptive responding:

- **Structure.** How is the piece organized? ("No organization" is not an option. Every piece has at least a beginning, middle, and end.)

- **Voice.** Describe the voice you hear (objective, tentative, whispering).

- **Point of View.** What is the position or stance on the subject? Is the author objective? Is he speaking as an involved participant? First, second, or third person?

- **Attitude toward the Reader.** How does the author treat the reader (condescending? pleading?)

- **Level of Abstraction or Correctness.** How much generalization? Detail? Example?

- **Language, Diction, Syntax.** What kinds of words are used? Jargon? Technical terms? Layman's? Metaphors and images? What kind of sentences and phrasing? Simple? Complex? (19)

These criteria are expansive and measure effective *communication*. They can easily be used as the basis of a rubric. Again, we must decide what we hope students will gain from the assignment. Our responses using these criteria will be a departure from grading because we will not be checking for content only.

Analytic responding would work for persuasive or argument papers. Elbow and Belanoff suggest the following criteria for feedback:

- **Reasons and Support.** What is the main point/claim/assertion of the whole paper? What are the reasons or points given? What support, backing, or argument is given? What support could be given? What are the counterargument(s) against the reason(s)?

- **Assumptions.** What assumptions does the paper seem to make? What does the paper take for granted?

- **Audience.** Who is the implied audience? Who is the writer talking to? What kind of readers would accept the reasons presented? What kind of reader would reject them? How does the writer treat the audience? as enemies? friends? equals? children? What is the writer's stance toward the audience? (27–28)

Notice that these criteria also compel us to look at the actual writing as a way of communicating. The emphasis here is on how well the author made his argument.

This way of thinking about student work may be very challenging for us. If we make the effort to view our students as communicators of knowledge, they will feel more pride in their work and view themselves as contributors to the collected knowledge of mankind. We may even see them display more pleasure toward our assignments.

## "We Are Coaches"

Giving feedback on students' writing in research assignments can be very time consuming, but it is so worth doing. I said before that the final paper should never be the first one we see—by then, it's too late for our students to learn from missteps. Kelly Gallagher, quoting Douglas Reeves, compares the feedback process to coaching an athlete. As the match goes on, the player goes to the sidelines for guidance, where coaches offer up a variety of strategies. Ultimately, the player chooses which ones to use and where and when to apply them (Gallagher 2006, 148). Our students should be allowed the same choice in their learning, particularly in writing and research. Our responses, therefore, must relate to *their* choices rather than our hope to see our own content reflected at us.

Linda Rief provides many suggestions and guidance on feedback in her book *Read Write Teach,* and she too considers the role of the coach. In observing her grandsons' coaches, she began "paying attention to [the way the coaches] talked to their players on the field and on the court" (2014, 157). Rief noticed a pattern to the coaches' responses:

> A positive comment—a pat on the back. A suggestion—a way to overcome the weakness. The opportunity to try again. As teachers, we are always trying to nurture growth. We are coaches. I want to be the teacher and the coach . . . who finds the positive, suggests alternatives and strategies, and gets out of the way to let the child play. (2014, 158)

This kind of response to and feedback on our students' work fosters a "growth mindset" (Dweck 2006, 15–17) rather than a punitive atmosphere.

# Chapter 7

## Making the Argument

*The important thing is not to stop questioning.*

—Albert Einstein

*In order to be irreplaceable, one must always be different.*

—Coco Chanel

So, how does all of this relate to our students and the awesome jobs we have in education? You may be shaking your head, wondering if I've totally lost it. It's impossible, what I ask. There's no time. It doesn't fit the curriculum. What about content? It's too hard to get students to do the work.

Kids must learn how to ask probing questions, find information—the good stuff—analyze situations logically, and create solutions. I don't say that lightly.

Self-advocacy, agency, confidence in decision making: these are all by-products and benefits of research skills. Citizens who educate themselves, who can broaden and narrow subject matter, who develop awareness of when more information is needed, who question, read closely, spot and form argument, analyze, make connections, and synthesize are good citizens indeed.

In life, problems and situations often arise that need solutions—some immediate, some long-term. People who can foresee and determine problems, present options, and implement solutions—think, in other words—are valuable to society, companies of all sizes, and local and national government agencies.

When our students see themselves as creators of knowledge instead of merely consumers, they have reached the level of advanced literacy. They are ready to hone their skills in higher education or practice them in the world. They can draw on their own knowledge and experience with confidence, recognize where there are gaps in their knowledge, locate and access information, ask questions, question authorities, make connections and decisions, and use their voices. Interpretation needs expression. Grammar can be wrong; expression can't.

In this chapter, I will lay out my argument for the importance of making time in our classes to work on research skills more pointedly using three ideas: everyday problems, fake news, and the workplace of the future. There are many stories in this chapter—some personal, some universal. I've learned a lot as I've written this book and worked on my own practice, and I appreciate your staying with me on this journey.

## Problems

Life hands us problems. We don't often get to choose what or when.

As I write this piece, it is an anniversary. July 24 is a day we mark but don't celebrate. On July 24, 2008, a storm that was later identified as a Category 3 tornado passed over our property. Other than a darkened sky, we had no warning. Those who had access to the National Oceanic and Atmospheric Administration report had about an eight-minute edge. This tornado cut a fifty-three-mile swath through New Hampshire woodlands, killing one woman, damaging numerous homes, and leveling acres of trees. Tornadoes are rare in New Hampshire, and such a sustained and ferocious one was for the record books.

My daughters and I were home when the rain started. We did exactly what we shouldn't have: closed the windows. We should have headed for the basement with the dog and rosary beads. We heard loud wind. We watched furniture blow off the deck. The rain looked like the snow pattern of channels that don't come in on your television. Then *bump! Crack! Thump! Thud!* Every tree on our property toppled in ten seconds. And then it was over.

But our trouble was just beginning.

There were four trees on the roof that opened eleven puncture holes through which water poured, and branches protruded through the ceilings of two upstairs rooms. It was still raining. Outside the house, trees lay diagonally over other trees. They looked like green waves that had frozen as they lapped the front and back doors of the house. Our wooded lot was clear-cut. The smell of pine overwhelmed us. Christmas in July!

We were trapped in the house for a while because the transformer at the end of our driveway, all the power lines, and several trees were down in the road. We had no electricity.

Inside the house, we could see damage to the ceilings of a bathroom and bedroom upstairs. Our daughter Laura's room had to be evacuated because of ceiling and wall damage, so we set her up in our daughter Sarah's room. What we couldn't see were the broken roof trusses. The first priority was to stop any more water damage inside the house. Neighbors appeared with large tarps, and a contractor, who was scheduled to redo the siding on the house later that summer, came over to help us cover the whole roof.

One of the most amazing things to me was how quickly some people came out of the woodwork (almost literally) to "help" us. Within hours of the tornado striking, some men with chain saws walked over downed wires and trees and offered to remove the four trees from our roof. In our desperation to get the holes covered, we agreed to let them do this work, for which they demanded immediate payment. Later, we had to negotiate with the insurance company to get reimbursed for this cost. Insurance companies call it "neglect" if homeowners fail to prevent more damage from occurring after an "act of God"; we had no choice but to pay these men so we could get the roof covered as quickly as possible.

What we needed to know about was liability. What if someone came onto our property to help clean up and was injured? We would be liable, even though we were not responsible for the conditions. We had to say no to several friends and neighbors who came by with offers of help. That work was best left to professional loggers who carry their own insurance coverage.

Local, and some not-so-local, carpenters stuck their business cards in our mailbox. I got very good at interviewing them. When the time came to discuss money, they would present their estimates and then I would tell them what insurance would pay. One of them ran to the door in his haste to get away.

I have a colleague who tells me all the time that "kids don't know what they don't know." Let's just say that, when the tornado hit, we didn't know what we didn't know. We didn't know the extent of the damage or what it would take to repair it. What we *did* know was how to ask questions. We had to figure out who could help us. We contacted a neighbor who happens to be a forester. Fortunately, his family and home were spared from the effects of the tornado. He was a tremendous help and a font of information. He warned us about the unpredictable nature of fallen green trees, which can snap up unexpectedly when the weight of trees on top of them is removed. He initiated us into the language of logging and provided the names of reputable people in the business who could begin the three-year-long process of cleaning up after the storm. Among other lessons, we learned the following:

- The inflexible parameters of our homeowners' insurance

- The names, functions, and limitations of excavating and logging equipment

- That some people may try to capitalize on the misfortune of others

The importance of good questioning skills cannot be overemphasized. There is a distinction between asking good questions and questioning, and both skills are invaluable in any real-life situation. Being comfortable asking questions can save a person pain and money when problems arise.

A couple of years ago, I was at the hospital on a Tuesday morning with my daughter Sarah, then twenty-two, who was having an attack of appendicitis. The hospital was a teaching one, which means that several student interns of various levels and specialties came in, interviewed Sarah, made suggestions, ordered some scans or tests, and left, never to be seen again (except for the nurse on the floor who managed the flow of people as well as Sarah's comfort). We saw maybe half-a-dozen students over the course of the day. It appeared that they did not communicate with one another. I watched the action carefully; it was like a scene in an interactive play.

At one point, one of the interns ordered barium for a GI scan, so Sarah drank the barium preparation. Later, they determined that there was no need for the GI, so she didn't drink the second one.

That afternoon, they decided that Sarah needed to have her appendix removed, so we went upstairs to consult with the anesthesiologists. (I was allowed to stay because Sarah requested it; otherwise, I would have been sidelined by the Health Insurance Portability and Accountability Act law.)

As standard operating procedure (no pun intended) dictates, the doctor asked Sarah a series of questions including, "When was the last time you had something to eat or drink?" Sarah told him that it had been six o'clock the previous evening.

I waited. No one wants to be a helicopter mom.

Sarah didn't mention the barium.

So, I did. "She had a barium drink here at one thirty today."

The doctor whipped his head around and said, "What?" He checked the clipboard with Sarah's record on it. "Why isn't that on this sheet?!" He looked at the documents again. "Good thing you mentioned that!" Then he explained to Sarah that anything in the stomach can cause serious complications for people under anesthesia, including the risk of death by aspiration. In order to proceed with the surgery that day, the doctor had to alter his plans for administering Sarah's anesthesia based on that information.

I won't run down the list of unfortunate experiences I've had that taught me about pre-op protocol. It's sufficient to say that I knew I should question the authority figure about the barium. Sarah didn't know what I knew, but, because she was aware of her knowledge gap, she allowed me to stay with her and raise the question. Her understanding of her own need for additional information may have saved her life.

When I asked Sarah's permission to tell this story, we had a great conversation about literacy. Because of my history with surgery (I've had several over the course of my life), I did not feel intimidated by the doctor and therefore provided him with some important information that he was lacking. I have also been the caretaker of a sick child who was treated at an excellent teaching hospital, so when I saw all the players involved with Sarah's care that Tuesday, I knew the patient was the only one who could connect all the dots.

That day taught Sarah an important lesson, which she used a few months later when she found the courage to question a notice from her landlords saying that they'd be raising the rent at her apartment complex. On her own, she sent them a letter asking if she could be exempt from the increase; she argued that she'd proven herself an exemplary tenant, was never late with payments, and had no complaints lodged against her by other tenants. They granted her the exemption that year.

Too many people don't ask questions or are afraid to question those in authority. Practicing questioning and asking questions can help our students in real life, which is why it is so important for us to provide a safe place for them to exercise this skill. Questions can save people when their experience is lacking and their background knowledge is incomplete—when "they don't know what they don't know."

Awareness of knowledge gaps and being able to identify when there is a need for more information are signs of advanced literacy skills that we can help students develop using the research process. Recently, I have been studying project- or problem-based learning (PBL), which I mentioned briefly in Chapter 2. PBL is a student-centered approach in which students take the lead in an active learning experience. It provides another way for us to help students see where they have knowledge gaps. It's also a great method for students to practice the research process in a practical scenario. Students find problems that can be solved in their own communities or that they are curious about. These problems are actual challenges with real stakeholders, and students use a hands-on approach for solving them. PBL is not new, and you may already be using it in your curriculum and instruction delivery. Appendix B includes my review of the literature on PBL plus some pros and cons I compiled through my own reading.

## Fake News

In recent years, news has expanded to social media, where citizens can view and comment on items on a micro level—from what happened down the street to world events. So much news is available, at such a rapid pace, that people are becoming inured to the truth. Ennui has set in. Are we paying attention, or is it all just washing over us? Have we chosen to surround ourselves with opinions that echo our own, or do we consider opposing viewpoints? We have become unwary consumers.

News entered the entertainment arena when it became available around the clock. News is supposed to be a reporting of facts from the happenings of the day conducted in an objective manner. The commentators on twenty-four-hour cable news channels are not objective. Information access has exploded within the last twenty years, leading to a prevalence of left-or-right-leaning commentary and opinion on these channels. Endless parades of experts analyze what now passes for "news" through their particular political and social lenses hour after hour. Unfortunately, many people don't recognize this news as entertainment, which results in misconceptions.

One serious problem that can plague an unwary citizenry is the increased frequency and effectiveness of "fake news." Fake news has been around since the days of Benjamin Franklin, who liked to write and publish satire. In the 1800s, this was called "yellow journalism." It started as a battle between preeminent newsmen William Randolph Hearst and Joseph Pulitzer, who were competing to sell newspapers, and it was refined at the turn of the twentieth century by "muckrakers"—journalists who were alarmed by the power large corporations amassed and the suffering of workers at that time.

> Writing fiction, documentaries, and serialized articles, these socially concerned writers began to critically consider the corruption and exploitation involving large companies. The term "muckrakers" was coined by President Theodore Roosevelt (1858–1919) in 1906 in reference to their ability to uncover "dirt." Roosevelt borrowed the word from John Bunyan's *Pilgrim's Progress* (1668), which spoke of a man with a "Muck-rake in his hand" who raked filth rather than

look up to nobler things. Later the presidential candidate for the Progressive Party in 1912, Roosevelt recognized the muckrakers' key role in publicizing the need for progressive reform but demanded that they know when to stop in order to avoid stirring up radical unrest. (Black 2006)

The key difference between the muckrakers and the fake news peddlers of today is the motive behind their work. Our press was instituted to inform the public of what transpires in government so that citizens can question and hold leaders accountable. Today's fake news creators operate on a base level with the intention of duping the public.

## News in the Eye of the Beholder?

Present-day journalists are not required to be licensed, but they do espouse and operate under a code of ethics adopted by the Society of Professional Journalists (SPJ). The code includes four basic tenets:

> *Seek truth and report it.* Ethical journalism should be accurate and fair. Journalists should be honest and courageous in gathering, reporting and interpreting information;

> *Minimize harm.* Ethical journalism treats sources, subjects, colleagues and members of the public as human beings deserving respect;

> *Act independently.* The highest and primary obligation of ethical journalism is to serve the public;

> *Be accountable and transparent.* Ethical journalism means taking responsibility for one's work and explaining one's decisions to the public. (1996)

Each tenet includes several principles that serve as guidance in anticipated circumstances or situations, such as "avoid conflicts of interest," "acknowledge mistakes and correct them promptly and prominently," and "never deliberately distort facts or context" (Society of Professional Journalists 1996).

It's not that we've never seen the press take a distinct stand on an issue or call for policy change over the course of history. Indeed, freedom of the press in this country must be protected at all costs as a measure against tyranny. This protection is exactly what the Founding Fathers intended when they provided for it under the Constitution.

The trouble now is that anyone with a device and an Internet connection can look like a journalist. A person with a smartphone can document news as it is happening and become a "citizen journalist" (Dugan 2008, 801). I recently saw a news item about "patient dumping" online. Imamu Baraka, a man on the street in Baltimore, witnessed hospital personnel wheeling a woman out of the hospital and leaving her on the sidewalk—in thirty-degree weather—clad in nothing but a hospital gown and socks. He caught this incident on video using his cell phone and alerted authorities, who returned her to the hospital (Cox, Vargas, and Moyer 2018).

Baraka posted his video of the incident on Facebook, where it was viewed more than 2.3 million times and sparked moral outrage. The *Washington Post* picked up the story and circulated a legitimate news article about patient dumping that included more details about the woman involved, comments from hospital administrators, other incidents of this phenomenon occurring across the country, and observations about the apparent breakdown of municipal systems in Baltimore, citing the death of Freddie Gray in 2015 and recent images of "Baltimore students bundled in coats in unheated schools" (Cox, Vargas, and Moyer 2018). I cannot say whether this *Washington Post* story has been read by 2.3 million people, but I doubt it. Facebook and other social networking sites have become news media outlets, whether they like it or not. Anyone with an account can present news-like content that others can comment on and spread at lightning speed.

Our students have front-row seats to this spectacle. We must be sure that our students understand and get lots of practice with evaluating sources for accuracy and authority and that they have an aptitude for spotting and forming argument. Citizen journalists are not beholden to the same ethical practices as professional journalists (Dugan 2008). As I write this chapter, our country is embroiled in a debate over how much of a role fake news played in our last presidential election. Getting our students to higher-order thinking while searching for information is paramount. We must break them of the notion that research is nothing more than finding answers and show them that there is a serious process involved that includes vetting sources for authority and accuracy, and close reading of information.

Fake news is insidious. It appears to be real because of its plausible subject matter and format. It's so real-looking that on occasion, legitimate news outlets have run fake news stories. Chris Berdik, writing for *Quill*, a journal of the SPJ, recounts an incident with a story about proposed plans for a "cemetery amusement park featuring gaudy memorials designed by artists, roller coasters, a souvenir shop, and refreshments at 'Dante's Grill'"

As an important aside, we need to inform our students that fake news is exactly that: fake. It is not a term to be used for legitimate news or for information with which we disagree. The term *fake news* has been applied in this context by politicians and others, and it is an incorrect characterization. Using the term *fake news* in this manner conflates truth and bias, effectively discrediting opposing viewpoints. We must insist on healthy discourse in our classrooms, and that includes how we handle disagreement or counterargument on any given issue. Please see the section on argument on page 164.

(2002, 1). The story was picked up by the Associated Press, *Los Angeles Times, Boston Herald,* and several smaller news outlets before they learned it was a satirical hoax written by Joey Skaggs, an artist who later sent out a press release declaring himself the creator of the fiction (2).

This story is an older one; the incident took place in 1999, when the Internet was relatively new, and well before the proliferation of smartphones and social media. Skaggs was not into fake news for money. He seemed to view it as sport, revealing all in the end for his apparent amusement. These days, fake news creators are a different breed.

On an *All Things Considered* segment on NPR, Laura Sydell attempted to expose the creator of a fake news story titled "FBI Agent Suspected in Hillary Email Leaks Found Dead in Apparent Murder-Suicide." Unlike Skaggs, the person(s) who wrote this fiction did not want to be found. When a routine search failed to unearth the author(s), the show enlisted the services of an engineer at a tech company in Berkeley, California. Sydell compared him to an archaeologist who dug deep into the web, finally discovering an e-mail address and eventually a name connected to it: Jestin Coler. They went to Coler's house in a Los Angeles suburb. Coler answered the door wearing "a heavy mesh steel screen" to cover his face and refused to speak about his company, Disinfomedia. He later agreed to an interview, where he said he got into the fake news business—and yes, it is a business—in 2013 "to highlight the extremism of the white nationalist alt-right" (Sydell 2016).

Coler has written fake news stories for other audiences as well. He referenced one about "how customers in Colorado marijuana shops were using food stamps to buy pot." That story resulted in a state legislator introducing a bill "to prevent people from using their food stamps to buy marijuana," which had never actually happened. When pressed, Coler admitted that he makes between $10,000 and $30,000 per month from his fake news business. The money comes from advertisers who buy space on his sites (Sydell 2016).

I include this story to emphasize the point that our students are swimming in this nebulous environment every day and that it is really easy for anyone to get hoodwinked by fake news. A study by the Stanford History Education Group (2016) showed that students from middle school through college displayed a shocking inability to distinguish fake news from real news. School-age students from both low and high socioeconomic areas, as well as students at six universities, from highly selective schools to state universities, across twelve states were given several dozen tasks and assessed on their performance. The sample included 7,804 responses. The findings of this study revealed the following:

> Overall, young people's ability to reason about the information on the Internet can be summed up in one word: *bleak*.

> When it comes to evaluating information that flows through social media channels, they are easily duped.

> By high school, we would hope that students reading about gun laws would notice that a chart came from a gun owner's political action committee. And, in 2016, we would hope college students, who spend hours each day online, would look beyond a .org URL and ask who's behind a site that presents only one side of a contentious issue. But in every case and at every level, we were taken aback by students' lack of preparation.

> Ordinary people once relied on publishers, editors, and subject matter experts to vet the information they consumed. But on the unregulated Internet, all bets are off. (2016, 4)

We certainly have our work cut out for us. Coler, the fake news creator, told NPR that these stories are not going to stop anytime soon, that they will just get more sophisticated and more difficult to distinguish from real news (Sydell 2016). How do we combat this threat? First, we have to tell students that these stories and their creators actually exist. Next, we can have students fact-check all sources that don't have well-known authors or corporate sponsors. Some suggest that we should adopt universal precautions toward any information we read on the unadulterated Internet, and social media especially. *Universal precautions* is a term used in the medical field in reference to biohazards such as bodily fluids and blood. All biohazards are approached as if they are infectious. Protective clothing and equipment are always used when handling them. If we were to apply this idea to material online, we would have to handle *everything* we see there as suspicious. This is an extreme approach. If we know where and how to look for it, information online is not only incredibly accessible but potentially excellent. I recommend thinking like a librarian instead.

## Thinking Like a Librarian

As a librarian in a secondary school, I develop the library collection based on four major factors (and many minor ones): quality (which includes authority and reputation), bias (or agenda), relevance, and appropriateness. Thousands of books are published each year. How do I decide which ones make the cut? Author reputation figures largely into my decisions. Has the author's body of work and experience shown her to be an excellent resource—for example, Jane Goodall or Rachel Carson? What are the author's credentials? Does the author have an extreme bias or agenda? Is there an organization financially backing the author? What does this organization support? Does the book or database support our curriculum and lend relevance to the collection? There are no books in our library without a named author. No author, no purchase.

I want students to "find their own truths," as Don Murray so eloquently said. I am cognizant that there is always some degree of bias in writing, but I avoid purchasing materials that deal with subjects from a radical or extremist viewpoint. For example, I would buy a book about animal rights, but not one produced by PETA. I also purchase material from reputable publishers. Going to the well-known, tried-and-true places for print and electronic resources greatly reduces the chances of receiving incorrect or biased products.

For all intents and purposes, when students are locating and accessing information they are amassing a small collection. At a minimum, we must teach and prompt students to look for an author or corporate sponsor when they conduct their research. This requirement is for writing in any format: print, online, tweet, bathroom wall. Thinking like a librarian could be a handy approach to this work:

- **Author or corporation** (preferably with a good reputation)—This is a must.
- **Potential bias**—Who is paying for the work to be produced, and why?
- **Relevance**—Does the information fit or enhance the subject under study?
- **Appropriateness**—Where does the information come from? (For example, www. cdc.gov is a much more reliable site than www.naturalnews.com.) Is the material suitable for the project?

Our students need to understand that the evaluation and close reading of information they locate must be done every time. Jeff Maehre explains this idea in his article "What It Means to Ban Wikipedia: An Exploration of the Pedagogical Principles at Stake":

> It seems to me that professors put too much emphasis on the *source* rather than the *information itself*. A journal article might be "better," overall, than a Wikipedia entry on the same subject, but how does that disqualify a particular piece of info that is mined from the latter? I always hear the sentence "we want them using the best sources." This may be reasonable enough, but it can come only from a conception of the research paper as a product rather than a learning tool, which in turn conceives of the student as a producer rather than as a learner . . . In short, I don't think what is important is that the student use the best sources. What *is* important is that the student *learn how to determine* the best source. (2009, 230–231)

Students may have to adapt their evaluation criteria to fit the purpose of the information-seeking activity; therefore, using stock criteria such as the CRAAP Test (O'Connor et al. 2010) is not necessarily useful for every research project. A dead giveaway that students should question a site's validity as a source is if the site solicits or accepts donations.

Figure 7.1 shows an article from a website that looks legitimate.

The Pacific Northwest Tree Octopus site has become somewhat famous. A teacher created and posted this site to teach his students a lesson about questioning information found online. Notice there are no sources attributed on this page, but it is colorful and text dense, making it look authoritative. Science terms and pictures are included as well. Unwary people viewing this site might believe that there are species of octopus that live in trees if they never ask any questions. We can find examples of sites from organizations that present plenty of great-looking information online—information that unfortunately is being used to lure potential customers. Legal firms, for example, often produce sites that look very sharp and may contain bulleted information that can be easily copied and pasted.

**ZPi** / Blog / New / FAQ

**ALUMINUM FOIL DEFLECTOR BEANIE**
The book THEY don't want you to read

| About | HELP! | FAQs | Sightings | Media |
| Activities | Links |

# THE PACIFIC NORTHWEST TREE OCTOPUS

The Pacific Northwest tree octopus (*Octopus paxarbolis*) can be found in the **temperate rainforests** of the Olympic Peninsula on the west coast of North America. Their habitat lies on the Eastern side of the Olympic mountain range, adjacent to Hood Canal. These solitary cephalopods reach an average size (measured from arm-tip to mantle-tip,) of 30-33 cm. Unlike most other cephalopods, tree octopuses are amphibious, spending only their early life and the period of their mating season in their ancestral aquatic environment. Because of the

Rare photo of the elusive tree octopus

moistness of the rainforests and specialized skin adaptations, they are able to keep from becoming desiccated for prolonged periods of time, but given the chance they would prefer resting in pooled water.

An intelligent and inquisitive being (it has the largest brain-to-body ratio for any mollusk), the tree octopus explores its arboreal world by both touch and sight. Adaptations its ancestors originally evolved in the three dimensional environment of the sea have been put to good use in the spatially complex maze of the **coniferous Olympic rainforests**. The challenges and richness of this environment (and the intimate way in which it interacts with it,) may account for the tree octopus's advanced behavioral development. (Some evolutionary theorists suppose that "arboreal adaptation" is what laid the groundwork in primates for the evolution of the human mind.)

## CEPHALONEWS

**2017-12-27 A New Species Of Giant Octopus Has Been Hiding In Plain Sight**
(Earther)
Some previously assumed Giant Pacific Octopuses (*Enteroctopus dofleini*) have been found to be a separate species, recently dubbed the Frilled Giant Octopus.

**2017-11-24 Toys Wanted For Scarborough Octopus**
(Yorkshire Coast Radio)
Sea Life Scarborough is appealing for toys for Barbara the giant Pacific Octopus. The centre wants the public's help to fill their octopus' advent calendar with a toy every day in the run up to Christmas.

**2017-11-14 Accident & Intent In An Octopuses' Garden**
(ABC.net.au)
"We recently published a scientific report of octopuses living together in unusual numbers at a site on the south coast of New South Wales. Then things got a little out of hand... Octlantis is not a city, and no artworks, fences, or buildings have been made."

**Figure 7.1** Pacific Northwest Tree Octopus site (courtesy of Lyle Zapato, zapatopi.net)

We can teach students to look for the purpose behind a web page by having them search for who posted or sponsored the site. This information is usually located at the very bottom of the web page. Purpose is significant. Some .org sites exist to raise awareness but also funding; they might post information and statistics taken from legitimate studies, but it could be only the information they think will net the best results for their bottom line. In other words, they might cherry-pick the information they present to best suit their organizational purpose. If original research studies or data are referenced on a site, students can be taught to locate this information and read the findings so they can draw their own conclusions. I often remind my students that all of the information on websites is put there by humans, and not all of those humans care about them.

## Advertisements

The recent Stanford study points out that students have difficulty distinguishing between advertisements and articles on websites. More than 80 percent of the respondents failed to recognize "native advertisement" and mistook it for news content (Stanford History Education Group 2016, 10). Companies make their material look important and as much like articles as possible to dupe people into reading it. Students, often looking for quick answers, are drawn in by the catchy headline and fail to see the words *sponsored content*. Marketers set snares; our students are caught.

We can help alleviate these mistakes by teaching students to look carefully at material, particularly online, although these "feature length" advertisements appear in print magazines too. They should look all around the edges of an article for language that might indicate an ad, such as "advertisement" or "sponsored material." Even information on databases may be one-sided. Research studies are routinely funded by organizations to provide empirical evidence to support their claims. Making note of the bias or agenda of those funding studies is worthwhile for yourself as well as your students.

Another thing we can do as teachers to help students with evaluating sources is to commit to the time it will take to do this work. Giving students only a week to do real research will force them to cut corners and seek quick answers from material they won't read closely. They won't learn or discover anything if they don't read and analyze the material. (See Chapter 4.) To make students aware of the extent to which they should view and evaluate sources, I developed a lesson that includes a game called Fake News: Are You at Least as Smart as a Librarian? In this game, students compete in a search for good websites on various topics (see Figure 7.2). The premise behind this lesson is

Fake News: Are You at Least as Smart as a Librarian?

Lesson objectives:    Students will demonstrate ability in evaluating sources
                      Students will demonstrate understanding of how to recognize false info
                      Students will demonstrate ability in discerning online advertisements

Method:               - Before class begins, have students put topic words or phrases on scrap
                        paper pieces and collect them

                      -Discuss the issue of "fake news"
                        - Its history (Yellow Journalism and Muckrakers)
                        - How to recognize advertisements and tell them apart from information
                        - Curriculum tie-in to Civics (What Do Judges Do?)

                      - Discuss how librarians make decisions about what goes in the collection
                      - Critical Thinking - the missing piece of research
                        - **Author or corporation** must be visible (and reputable)
                        - **Beware of bias** - who is paying for the work to be produced and why?
                          Are the views expressed extremist (politically or religiously)?
                        - **Relevance** - does the information fit or enhance the subject of study?
                        - **Reliability** - where are you getting your information?
                          www.cdc.gov is much more reliable than www.naturalnews.com
                        - Does the site gladly accept Visa or Mastercard?
                        - Does it say "Sponsored" or "Donate" anywhere on the site?

Play the game "Are You at Least as Smart as a Librarian?"

Pick three pairs of contestants to play. Use the screen and the LCD projector to bring up the
Internet, specifically Google. Draw a topic out of a hat at random (from the collection you took
up from the students at the beginning of class). Type the topic word into the search box so the
audience can see it, but the pairs of contestants should have their own computers to work with.

Contestants search the first page of hits for a good source on that topic that meets librarian
criteria. Ten points for the first group that finds an excellent source. If none can be found, then
students can add other search terms and try again. Contestants need to write down the extra
search term(s) used. Five extra points for the team that adds a successful search term and finds an
excellent source on the second try for a total of 15 for that round. The winning pair stays and then
two more pairs are picked to compete for the second round. Go until everyone has had a chance to
play.

**Figure 7.2** Fake News: Are You at Least as Smart as a Librarian?

that if students are going to bypass the vetted material in the library in favor of the open Internet, they must be at least as smart as the librarian. I have taught this lesson a few times, and it is an eye-opener. It also generates a lot of questions.

## Determining the Problem and Presenting an Argument

One of the main reasons we begin research with questions and background reading is to determine whether there is an issue or a problem, and what that issue is, before we start to form an argument. For example, the Colorado legislator who brought the bill barring people from using food stamps to purchase marijuana (see page 158) could have saved himself a lot of effort if he had simply looked for any other information in print on this issue. If he really wanted to do due diligence, he could have surveyed businesses to learn whether people were in fact using their public assistance for that purpose. Using those data, he could have determined exactly how much of a problem it was (or wasn't), and as a result he could have spent his time and energy on actual pressing issues. Our students can conduct the same kind of preliminary inquiry, especially if they are arguing about issues of policy. What they believe to be a problem might not be. However, students haven't failed if they find no problem. They've learned something very valuable: to put reason before emotion when pursuing a line of inquiry.

It is extremely important for *all* students to possess information literacy skills, not just college-bound students. Frequently in the ebb and flow of life, it is necessary to present an argument (one that contains more substance than which sports team is better than others); it is equally necessary to be able to identify an argument when one is being leveled at you.

Mastering the research process is a great way to acquire or hone the skills needed for presenting and identifying argument. Argument is addictive, and teens are very capable of forming a good argument. Have you ever witnessed a teen making his case for borrowing the car—the new one—on a Saturday night, or imploring her parents to let her hang out with friends past ten o'clock on a school night? Students are naturals at this. It is up to us to show them that their awesome parent-manipulation skills are transferrable to school assignments.

Argument can be a great way for our students to learn content. We can also teach our students the specific language and parts of argument, thereby accomplishing two things at once. In an academic setting, rules of engagement apply to argument. These rules can differ from discipline to discipline and can vary depending upon purpose, as in arguments of judgment versus arguments of policy. Argument can elicit emotional responses and may involve ethical considerations as well.

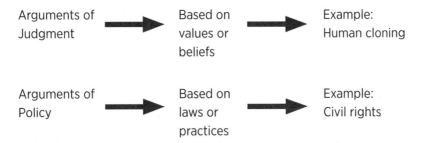

If we are going to assign research, which always includes a claim or thesis statement, then we need to teach students the language associated with academic argument, its structure, its parts, and the functions of each part. We also have to prepare students for how to utilize and navigate the ethical, emotional, and logical considerations that go along with argument building and delivery: *ethos* (appealing to a sense of right and wrong), *pathos* (playing on feelings), and *logos* (appealing to logical considerations).

Argument and persuasion are subtle forms of manipulation, and students should see them as such. To teach this concept, I use an editorial I found on readwritethink. org about the dangers of selfies. The piece is rhetorical, and it's filled with anecdotes and images of people putting themselves in harm's way in an effort to capture the scene on their cell phones. Here are the first few paragraphs:

> All too frequently, common sense takes a holiday with a cellphone in hand.
>
> According to the National Safety Council, an estimated 1.6 million accidents occur annually as distracted drivers text. The University of North Texas Health Science Center has determined 16,141 deaths occurred as a result of texting while driving.
>
> Those are frightening statistics for anyone on the road who could become the victim of such wanton negligence.
>
> But the dangers in the digital divide don't stop there. In this Age of Internet Narcissism, dozens of deaths annually have been attributed to selfies—self-portraits using cellphones often taken in unusual circumstances.
>
> A North Carolina driver was killed when she crashed into a truck while posting a selfie of herself singing Pharrell Williams' "Happy." . . . (Courier Editorial Staff 2015)

Invariably the irony of this story strikes some students as funny, and they laugh out loud. At that point, I bring to their attention that they've been manipulated. Most of them wouldn't have laughed if the author had simply said that the driver died when she took a selfie while driving her car. The author employed effective writing by pointing out the juxtaposition of an unflaggingly upbeat song playing at the time of a fatal car crash. Students can visualize the young woman singing at the top of her lungs, alone in her car, and wanting to preserve the moment in a photograph. It is a relatable scenario for them. During this lesson, I contrast the writing style of this editorial piece with an example of an academic argument so my students can note the differences.

Our students receive argument writing assignments frequently, but many do not fully understand the makeup of a good argument. George Hillocks Jr., in his book *Teaching Argument Writing, Grades 6–12*, supplies this description of the parts of argument:

> Toulmin's basic conception of argument includes several elements:
>
> - a claim
>
> - based on evidence of some sort
>
> - a warrant that explains how the evidence supports the claim
>
> - backing supporting the warrants
>
> - qualifications and rebuttals or counterarguments that refute competing claims (2011, xix)

One of my favorite examples of spontaneous argument occurs at the opening of an episode of the television show *The Big Bang Theory* (2008). The physicists are situated around their usual table at Cal Tech's cafeteria, and they are discussing whether Superman's perspiration exhibits his otherworldly powers. (Does Superman even sweat?) All the parts of argument are there: claim, evidence, warrant, backing, and rebuttals (Hillocks 2011). The four participants are engaged, animated, and passionate as they offer their evidence for and against the claim that Superman's sweat is infused with his superpowers.

The premise of this scene is silly, but isn't this level of passion and engagement for a subject what we are all hoping our students achieve? Imagine if students lost themselves in deep discussion and debate on the American Revolution . . . there would be no stopping them!

As I said in Chapter 1, if we want more than a report out of student research assignments, we must show students how facts can be used to support their thinking. Argument is another application of this concept. When writing an argument or a persuasive paper, a quote, summary, or paraphrase from a source cannot stand alone (see Chapter 5). Additional information must be included that explains why and how the evidence supports the claim. The supporting information is where the warrants and backing come in, making the claim stronger.

Argument is kind of a sticky wicket. It can raise emotions—sometimes by design, as I mentioned earlier. Who isn't moved by the sight of a sickly and emaciated puppy while Sarah McLachlan croons "In the Arms of an Angel" in the background? Many of us reach for our wallets before the phone number for the animal rescue even appears on the TV screen. This argument jerks on the heartstrings; logic is notably absent. That strategy works in commercials and campaigns, but in academic writing, we expect argument to be rooted in logic and ethics rather than emotion. Tom Romano speaks of this idea when he says, "If our decisions are to be both sound and humane, we need to understand emotion and circumstance, as well as logic and outcome" (2000, 57). Feelings play a part in any argument—even one about Superman's sweat—but the key word here is *understand*. There are times when reason must weigh more in the balance than emotion.

Judgment often comes from beliefs or values, which can be tied to emotion—particularly when there is an ethical concern, as in the case of human cloning. One might agree with an argument against cloning humans on ethical grounds but may consider a logical argument on the subject. Policies and laws are made by combining ethics and logic. Most people believe that murder is wrong, so there are laws against it and policies on how to deal with murder when it occurs that likely take into account the feelings of everyone involved.

In our current environment of fake news, emotionally charged responses to public figures and policy, nonstop political commentary, and a seeming unwillingness of people to hear or consider opposing viewpoints, it is more important than ever that our students understand how argument works, how to form and use argument, and how to recognize when argument is being used to influence them. In addition, students will learn our content much more thoroughly if they examine both sides of an argument using reason and logic.

Many excellent resources exist for teaching argument writing; here are three:

*Teaching Arguments: Rhetorical Comprehension, Critique, and Response* by Jennifer Fletcher

*Write Like This: Teaching Real-World Writing Through Modeling & Mentor Texts* by Kelly Gallagher

*Teaching Argument Writing, Grades 6–12* by George Hillocks Jr.

# Bring on the Bots

We have all heard, and likely read, so much about twenty-first-century skills and may still have no clear understanding of what it all means—at least I don't. Technology is certainly a very big part of living in the twenty-first century, but it isn't everything, as some would have us believe. Man has long created tools to assist with living, and we have been automating work functions for two centuries. Just think of the household chores that are now performed by machines: laundry, washing dishes, and cooking, for example. What happened when women no longer had to bring the washing to the river and beat it against rocks? Their time was freed up considerably, allowing them to take on other activities such as entering the workplace. This change didn't happen overnight—it took decades for women to become a real force at work outside their homes. There is a markedly faster pace to the changes we experience today, and that may be what alarms or excites us about the twenty-first century.

The US Bureau of Labor Statistics has projected trends for the immediate future of the world of work. In an essay titled "Expect 25 Years of Rapid Change," Hassett and Strain suggest that by the year 2040, the workplace will see three distinct trends. First, people will retire at a much older age, keeping them in the workforce into their seventies. Second, work will become more "task" oriented, with people working as independent contractors and hiring themselves out to perform varied tasks on their own terms and schedule; the authors cite Uber as a model of this type of task-oriented work concept. In this scenario, there is no regular place or organization to which people will report every day. Third, "intelligent robots" will hit the workforce. As they put it, "Your heart surgeon will still have a beating heart—though she will likely be assisted by a tin man" (2016, 1).

These projections are similar to everything I've seen about the twenty-first-century workplace. There are also indicators that other qualities will be valuable for employees to possess—such as "social skills, which Pew Research Center defines as encompassing interpersonal skills, written and spoken communication skills, and management or leadership skills" (Desilver 2016)—because jobs requiring these abilities are going to increase in the future. There is no way to predict what the workplace, or work itself, will look like—even in the immediate future—so people will need to possess the ability to learn and relearn tasks and functions independently to succeed in tomorrow's world.

Although we have an unprecedented number of tools available for learning in this century, the skills needed to make best use of them were developed in the Middle Ages with the advent of scholasticism. Although scholasticism had its roots in religion, philosophy, and morality, the learning method students used was very similar to what we teach for research skills:

> The scholastic thinker set out a proposition to be debated and then he proceeded to present arguments on both sides of this question. He carefully answered each argument in support of this proposition and in each opposition before coming to a final conclusion about the matter . . . A thorough knowledge of the ideas of previous authorities was also a key skill needed by those students who hoped to succeed in mastering the method. The accomplished scholastic was expected not only to be able to deal with problems in their discipline logically, but to recall and manipulate the ideas of previous authorities on a subject. These skills were put to the test in oral debate, as students were called upon to demonstrate mastery of the material through engaging their peers in verbal matches. (Bleiberg et al. 2005)

Students who master research skills are truly prepared for the twenty-first-century workplace. If work is task oriented, then they will succeed using the ability to determine a need (market), learn what is necessary to perform the task(s), and then deliver the product(s) or service(s). Technology tools can help expedite this process, but literacy skills are going to carry the day—much like Michelangelo employing his chisel on a block of marble. If more machines are part of the workforce, then people should be able to bring their creativity to the job.

## Competing with the Bots

Bots can sift through tons of information at a quick rate, but they have no ability to conceptualize, intuit, or place a value on ideas. Philosophy escapes them completely, and so do ethical considerations. Artificial intelligence (AI) can only "process homogeneous data, i.e., that, 'which is present'" (Gasparyan 2016, 734). Machines cannot transcend, or "relate to the world from outside" (734), which humans do by drawing on that which lies within. This stark contrast is something we would do well to remember and point out often to students (and to the powers that be).

Computers can acquire "knowledge" in the sense that they can recognize patterns in data and retain that information, but they can't rank information by importance. The best way to illustrate this point is via a *Star Trek: The Next Generation* episode titled "In Theory," in which the character Data, an android (human-looking artificial intelligence life form), has a "romantic relationship" with a human woman, Jenna.

In a stilted scene, Data and Jenna have a date that gets somewhat physical:

> *Jenna: Kiss me.*
>
> *(They kiss.)*
>
> *Jenna: What were you just thinking?*
>
> *Data: In that particular moment, I was reconfiguring the warp field parameters, analyzing the collected work of Charles Dickens, calculating the maximum pressure I could safely apply to your lips, considering a new food supplement for Spot.*
>
> *Jenna: I'm glad I was in there somewhere. (1991)*

## Umami: The Spice of Life

Most of us have heard of umami—that hard-to-define taste sensation that hits the tongue after salty, sweet, sour, and bitter. In a workplace—or even a world—crowded with robots, humans are the umami. Plain white rice will fill and feed you, but add a little soy sauce and the rice becomes much more palatable. Humans possess some qualities that I hope AI never will. These include instinct, experience, intuition, self-preservation, ethics (ethos), compassion/empathy (pathos), judgment, guile, the ability to anticipate, adaptation, extemporaneous speech, dissatisfaction, metacognition, and humor.

Almost all human development and advancement has come about because of dissatisfaction. As of this writing, AI is driven by logic and therefore cannot theorize, construct knowledge, feel boredom, express a unique voice, or develop ideas. Analysis is a computational skill at which robots excel because of their unassailable logic. Synthesis, however, requires a hunch plus prior knowledge and experience combined with the results of analysis. My story about questioning the doctor about anesthesia illustrates this point (see page 152). A computer won't gamble. People will.

Recall the incident involving US Airways flight 1549 on January 15, 2009. The plane had barely taken off when a small band of Canada geese got sucked into its engines and stalled them. The pilot, Chesley Sullenberger (Sully), chose to land the plane on the Hudson River. His quick thinking, assessment, experience, and gut instinct saved all 155 people on board as well as the aircraft itself, with no damage to nearby property except for passenger baggage. Investigators pointed out that the computers onboard, and on the ground, calculated that the aircraft could have been flown to one or two nearby airports. Sully decided that the best option was to land on the Hudson, even though logic dictated he should land on the ground. Eventually, investigators concluded that the pilot made the right decision (Sullenberger and Zaslow 2009, 274). Sully drew on his vast experience and expertise and called an audible that withstood the scrutiny of the play review.

IBM has a famous "smart" computer called Watson that has been touted as the latest tool for doctors to help diagnose and create treatment plans for cancer patients. Watson is supplied with all of the latest facts, information, research studies, and even doctors' notes on patients; it "finds the correct answers" but does not transform the information. It can't make adjustments to include human variables such as patient medical history (Freedman 2017).

In 2011, Watson appeared on an episode of the TV game show *Jeopardy!* (the full episode is available for viewing on YouTube). The AI blew away its human competition, but what was it really doing? Retrieval of answers is a low-tier skill. Why should we be impressed by that?

Our students need to understand that the research process enables them to use the human qualities that allow them to question, think, transform information, learn new things, and grow. This ability will help them face whatever life has in store.

# Appendices

# Appendix A

**List of Topics by Category** (Adapted from Allen and Camille, *The Multigenre Research Paper*. Portsmouth, NH: Heinemann.)

## HISTORICAL EVENTS

Aftermath of Hiroshima
Alamo
Apollo 13
Atomic Bomb
Battle of Gettysburg
Battle of Midway
Berlin Wall
Blizzard of 1938
Blizzard of 1978
Civil Rights Movement
Cold War
D-Day
Declaration of Independence
Denmark in the Holocaust

Desert Storm
Discover of Penicillin
Exxon *Valdez*
Great Depression
*Hindenburg*
Holocaust
Hurricane Katrina
Integration
Irish Potato Famine
Italian Immigration
The Manhattan Project
Newsies' Strike
Oklahoma City Bombing
Pearl Harbor
Polio Vaccine

Racism
Roaring 20s
Salem Witch Trials
San Francisco Earthquake
September 11, 2001
Slavery
Space Shuttle
*Titanic*
Trojan War
Underground Railroad
USS *Arizona*
Vietnam War
Watergate
Women's Suffrage
Woodstock

## MUSICIANS

ABBA
Paula Abdul
Clay Aiken
Louis Armstrong
Beatles
Beethoven
Bono
Garth Brooks
Mariah Carey
Harry Chapin
Sean Combs
Miles Davis
Five Iron Frenzy
Jerry Garcia
Evelyn Glennie
Amy Grant

David Helfgott
Jimi Hendrix
Faith Hill
Lauryn Hill
Janet Jackson
Michael Jackson
Jewel
Billy Joel
Elton John
John Lennon
Liberace
Madonna
Bob Marley
Dave Matthews
Bette Midler
Jim Morrison

Mozart
Stevie Nicks
Elvis Presley
Queen
Selena
Tupac Shakur
Paul Simon
Jessica Simpson
Frank Sinatra
Lynyrd Skynrd
Spice Girls
Tina Turner
Steven Tyler
U2
Von Trapp Family

## ARTISTS

Sam Butcher
Mary Cassatt
Salvador Dali
Leonardo da Vinci
Walt Disney

Filippo Lippi
Manet
Michelangelo
Monet
Precious Moments

Rafaello
Norman Rockwell
Titian
Vincent van Gogh

## PHOTOGRAPHERS

| | | |
|---|---|---|
| Anne Geddes | William Wegman | Ansel Adams |

## DIRECTORS

| | | |
|---|---|---|
| Ron Howard | George Lucas | Steven Spielberg |

## INSPIRATION TO THE INDIVIDUAL WRITER

| | | |
|---|---|---|
| Alicia<br>Ambassador to Greece | Jacques Cousteau | Ryan White |

## SPORTS

| | | |
|---|---|---|
| Hank Aaron | Magic Johnson | Jackie Robinson |
| Tenley Albright | Michael Jordan | Gabbi Reece |
| Muhammad Ali | Nancy Kerrigan | Mary Lou Retton |
| Marcus Allen | Michele Kwan | Dennis Rodman |
| American Cheerleading | Tara Lapinski | Babe Ruth |
| America's Cup | Vince Lombardi | Joan Benoit Samuelson |
| Fred Bear | Mickey Mantle | Barry Sanders |
| Larry Bird | Dan Marino | Kelly Slater |
| Roger Clemens | Masters Tournament | Emmitt Smith |
| Roberto Clemente | Jeremy McGrath | John Stockton |
| John Elway | Joe Namath | Tiger Stadium |
| Fenway Park | Olympic Games | Antoine Walker |
| Lou Gehrig | Bobby Orr | Ted Williams |
| Wayne Gretsky | Jesse Owens | Serena Williams |
| Scott Hamilton | Walter Payton | Venus Williams |
| Sergei and Katerina | Steve Prefontaine | Tiger Woods |

## CURRENT EVENTS

| | | |
|---|---|---|
| Columbine High School | Bill Gates | 2004 Olympics |
| Ennis Cosby | John Gotti | Iraq War |
| Flight 800 | | |

## TOPICS OF INTEREST

| | | |
|---|---|---|
| Abortion | Barnum and Bailey, Ringling Brothers' Circus | Cloning |
| Adoption | | Clothing |
| Alcoholism | Ben and Jerry's Ice Cream | Computer Chip |
| Anorexia | Black Regiment of the Civil War | Disney World |
| Armadillos | | Divorce |
| Neil Armstrong | Cedar Point | Dolphins |
| Attention Deficit Disorder | Child Abuse | Dyslexia |
| Autism | Chocolate | Egypt |
| Barbie | | Ellis Island |

## TOPICS OF INTEREST (*Continued*)

ESL
F-117
Football
Dian Fossey
Bill Gates
Jane Goodall
Billy Graham
Harley Davidson
Hawaiian Luau
Jim Henson/*Sesame Street*
Milton Hershey
History of the Broadway
    Musical
History of the Car
History of Jazz
History of TV
Hummers
Jeeps
Internet

KFC and Colonel Sanders
Legos
Lincoln Memorial
Looney Tunes
Mardi Gras
Mary Kay Cosmetics
Microsoft
Motocross
Mud-Bugging
Multiple Sclerosis
Muscular Dystrophy
Native Americans
Neuroblastoma
Nutrition
Poverty
*Price Is Right*/Bob Barker
Punk Music
Rape
Raves

*Rug Rats*
*Saturday Night Live*
School Buses
Charles Schulz
Septuplets
*The Simpsons*
Skateboarding
Skin Cancer
Spider-Man
Spinal Cord Injuries
George Steinbrenner
Tattooing
Temporal Lobe Epilepsy
UFOs
Mount Washington
*Winnie the Pooh*
*The Wizard of Oz*
Witchcraft

## HISTORICAL FIGURES

Anastasia
Richard Byrd
Brunelleschi
Cleopatra
Copernicus
Princess Diana
Amelia Earhart
Thomas Edison
Albert Einstein
Queen Elizabeth
Henry Ford
King Francis I
Ben Franklin
Galileo
Mahatma Gandhi

Thomas Jefferson
JFK Jr.
Joan of Arc
Sir John Hawkwood
Nathan Hale
Harry Houdini
Helen Keller
Bobby Kennedy
Jackie Kennedy Onassis
John Kennedy
Genghis Khan
Martin Luther King Jr.
Queen Lili'uokalani
Abe Lincoln
Charles Lindbergh

Lorenzo de' Medici
Golda Meir
Machiavelli
Maria Montessori
Isaac Newton
Richard Nixon
Annie Oakley
Franklin Roosevelt
Sacajawea
Mother Teresa
Harriet Tubman
George Washington
Charles Whitman
Wright Brothers

## ACTORS

| | | |
|---|---|---|
| Fred Astaire | Judy Garland | Adam Sandler |
| Lucille Ball | Audrey Hepburn | Jimmy Stewart |
| Orlando Bloom | Gene Kelly | Shirley Temple |
| Marlon Brando | Jerry Lewis | Charlize Theron |
| Bill Cosby | Marilyn Monroe | John Travolta |
| Leonardo DiCaprio | Mary Tyler Moore | John Wayne |
| James Dean | Rosie O'Donnell | Oprah Winfrey |
| Chris Farley | Ginger Rogers | Reese Witherspoon |
| Michael J. Fox | | |

## WRITERS

| | | |
|---|---|---|
| Louisa May Alcott | Emily Dickinson | Dr. Seuss |
| Maya Angelou | Margaret Mitchell | Shakespeare |
| Bocaccio | Gary Paulsen | J. R. R. Tolkien |
| Lewis Carroll | | |

# Appendix B

# REVIEW OF THE LITERATURE ON PROBLEM-BASED LEARNING (PBL)

The idea of project/problem/product-based learning (PBL) was conceived more than a century ago by none other than the venerable John Dewey. In 1918, William Heard Kilpatrick, a student of Dewey's, expanded on Dewey's educational philosophy, added a little "contemporary psychological thought," and came up with "The Project Method," an essay he published in the fall of that year.

> In Kilpatrick's thinking, the goal of projects was to foster student motivation by encouraging students to freely decide the "purposes" they wanted to pursue. He believed that unless students were given unfettered voice and choice, schoolwork would only be drudgery, and this would alienate students and be counter-productive to the ultimate educational goal of producing productive citizens. (Larmer, Mergendoller, and Boss 2015, 26–27)

In response to perceived problems with the public educational system in the last four decades, PBL has had a resurgence of sorts as an alternative to the more traditional content-driven, teacher-led instructional models. As a result, there is a plethora of research studies available on the subject. Thus far, I have read eight of these, the subjects of which range from first grade to middle school to high school to undergraduate to graduate level. I found the following recurring themes:

- Structure—to what extent should teachers structure the projects/classroom environment
- Transfer of knowledge/skills/experiences to other learning situations
- Comfort zone issues for teachers and students (e.g., assessment, expectations, etc.)
- Correlation between learner autonomy/independence and increased knowledge and satisfaction with the process (e.g., reflective logs, students marking own progress, etc.)

## Structure

Several of the studies tackled the idea of structure. It is a scary concept to turn the learning and project management over to students completely, even graduate students. Much study has been done on the structuring of the classroom environment, instruction, and facilitation of projects. Do teachers select the groups? Do students decide on what questions or problems to pursue? Should there be instruction before the project begins, or do we allow students to determine and fill in their own knowledge gaps? How much support is too much?

Joham and Clarke (2012) found that "successful PBL is as dependent on providing appropriate levels of structure and support as it is on choosing an appropriate problem scenario" (87). Indeed, plenty of concern and debate exist about proper levels of structure in PBL opportunities. MacGregor and Thomas (2002) compared the outcomes when there were highly structured, teacher-directed, problem-solving activities in a project versus totally student-directed groups. They found that students who were in the teacher-directed groups "seemed to have a better understanding of the transformation concept" (8) and tended to work collaboratively, whereas those in the student-led groups assumed clearly defined roles and worked independently, expressing "a sense of self-confidence and pleasure with their accomplishments" (10–11).

For this review of the literature, I interpreted the role of the teacher within the PBL instructional model as structure. Chin and Chia (2004) reported a great effect when the teacher acted as a facilitator, keeping groups and students on task, planning actions, and redirecting students. Teachers behaved like "partners in education" rather than the keepers of knowledge (75). Mitchell, Foulger, Wetzel, and Rathkey (2009) observed a veteran first-grade teacher "integrate the standards into the children's interest, rather than vice-versa"; this same teacher "encouraged students to work together to solve their own problems" (345).

## Transfer of Knowledge

One of the goals of education is to have students identify learning situations where their previous knowledge and experiences can be applied. PBL allows for transfer of knowledge. Two of the studies made explicit mention of finding that students were able to transfer their knowledge: Joham and Clarke (2012) and Mitchell, Foulger, Wetzel, and Rathkey (2009). MacGregor and Thomas (2002) specifically mention metacognition (thinking about thinking) and integrating technology into the project. These findings are particularly exciting when it comes to secondary and postsecondary education.

## Comfort Zone Issues

PBL is a very different instructional model from the traditional lecture-lecture-lecture-lecture-test model. With PBL, teachers have to share or hand over the lead on instruction and learning. This idea can heighten anxiety for both teachers and students. Students, accustomed to more passive instructional models, may feel uncomfortable directing their own learning, something they might never have been asked to do at school. Teachers may feel discomfort with letting go of the reins in the classroom. Six of the eight studies I read specifically mentioned issues pertaining to comfort zone. Concerns included student anxiety regarding lack of direction; group dynamics (agreeing on meeting times, disagreements about next steps in research, delegating work, lack of cooperation); assessment methods; lack of organization; students deciding on the form of the presentation; student-oriented classrooms; mind-set of students (motivation, willingness to take responsibility for learning process); PBL takes time; people will have to change ingrained habits; lack of specific guidelines (Joham and Clarke 2012; Chin and Chia 2004; Marwan 2015; Garran 2008; Akhand 2015; Mitchell, Foulger, Wetzel, and Rathkey 2009).

## Correlation Between Learner Autonomy and Increased Knowledge

Despite the comfort zone issues, every single study I read about indicated positive outcomes from the implementation of PBL. Observations included students having to notice and fill in their own knowledge gaps; keeping reflective logs allowed students to mark their own progress; giving all students the same opportunities and challenges; overcoming setbacks; students constructing their own knowledge; students evaluating their own learning and progress; teachers needing to make fewer accommodations; students learning "appropriate emotional responses to success and failure in themselves and others"; students owning their work; placing a value on mistakes—i.e., they benefit all students, not just the one making the mistake (Joham and Clarke 2012; Chin and Chia 2004; Marwan 2015; Garran 2008; Akhand 2015; Mitchell, Foulger, Wetzel, and Rathkey 2009; Ajai and Imoko 2015; MacGregor and Thomas 2002).

Most of the studies mentioned record-keeping or reflective logs as being particularly useful for students, because they were able to chronicle their progress and make note of setbacks and successes.

## Conclusion

Implementing PBL requires open minds and patience. PBL is a very different, but not new, model of instruction that has many proven benefits. PBL allows students to improve and expand skills such as literacy, research, problem solving, and critical thinking. In addition, PBL offers other benefits such as improved work ethic, growth mind-set, grit, perseverance, and learning how to learn. Every one of these ideals and skills appears on our list of core values for our students.

## PBL Implementation Guides

Arlington Education and Employment Program. 1997. *Project Based Learning and Assessment: A Resource Manual for Teachers*. Arlington, VA: Arlington Public Schools.

Cooper, R., and E. Murphy. 2016. *Hacking Project Based Learning: 10 Easy Steps to PBL and Inquiry in the Classroom*. Cleveland, OH: Times 10.

Larmer, J., J. Mergendoller, and S. Boss. 2015. *Setting the Standard for Project Based Learning*. Alexandria, VA: ASCD.

Railsback, J. 2002. *Project-Based Instruction: Creating Excitement for Learning*. Portland, OR: Northwest Regional Educational Laboratory.

# References

Ajai, J. T., and I. I. Imoko. 2015. "Gender Differences in Mathematics Achievement and Retention Scores: A Case of Problem-Based Learning Method." *International Journal of Research in Education and Science* 1(1): 45–50.

Akhand, M. M. 2015. "Project Based Learning (PBL) and Webquest: New Dimensions in Achieving Learning Autonomy in a Class at Tertiary Level." *Pan-Pacific Association of Applied Linguistics* 19(2): 55–74.

Chin, C., and L. Chia. 2004. "Implementing Project Work in Biology Through Problem-Based Learning." *Journal of Biological Education* 38(2): 69–75.

Garran, D. K. 2008. "Implementing Project-Based Learning to Create 'Authentic' Sources: The Egyptological Excavation and Imperial Scrapbook Projects at the Cape Cod Lighthouse Charter School." *The History Teacher* 41(3): 379–389.

Joham, C., and M. Clarke. 2012. "Teaching Critical Management Skills: The Role of Problem-Based Learning." *Teaching in Higher Education* 17(1): 75–88.

Larmer, J., J. Mergendoller, and S. Boss. 2015. *Setting the Standard for Project Based Learning*. Alexandria, VA: ASCD.

MacGregor, S. K., and W. R. Thomas. 2002. "Learning Geometry Dynamically: Teacher Structure or Facilitation?" National Educational Computing Conference Proceedings, San Antonio, Texas, June 17–19.

Marwan, A. 2015. "Empowering English Through Project-Based Learning with ICT." *The Turkish Online Journal of Educational Technology* 14(4): 28–37.

Mitchell, S., T. S. Foulger, K. Wetzel, and C. Rathkey. 2009. "The Negotiated Project Approach: Project-Based Learning Without Leaving the Standards Behind." *Early Childhood Education* 36: 339–346.

# PBL Pros and Cons

| Pros | Cons |
|---|---|
| Makes student work visible to the community | Not content driven; students have more control over direction in the classroom |
| Real, authentic projects that could benefit many | Challenging (but not impossible) to assess |
| Application of knowledge/skills to things that really matter | Possibly moving away from traditional grading |
| People see immediate return on investment | Different instructional model |
| Student engagement on all levels | Emphasizes depth over breadth |
| Relevance | Students will be out of comfort zone |
| Demonstrates our belief in grit, perseverance, self-efficacy and agency, growth mind-set, and work ethic | Teachers will be out of comfort zone |
| Students learn how to learn | Interpersonal problems may emerge |
| Students learn how to overcome setbacks | Needs to be implemented in multiple places to be most effective |
| Opportunity to transfer knowledge/skills/ experiences to new learning situations | Will require professional development |
| Self-reflections (notes kept by students during process) can show students' progress | |
| Students must acquire/fill in own knowledge | |
| Students improve literacy and research skills | |
| Employs skills and important concepts (e.g., audience, critical thinking, stakeholders, research, problem solving, speaking, collaboration, teamwork) | |
| Tangible results/product (something other than a paper) | |
| Improves motivation; students derive pleasure from learning | |
| Emphasizes depth over breadth | |

# Appendix C

Mr. Troendle

Freshmen Seminar Period 2

16 October 2017

Criticizing Censorship Control

As a female teenager in today's society one of the most debated and anger intensifying conversations in school is dress code. Dress code for me and many others is an annoyance. Seemingly small things like crop tops, shorts and tank top straps have restrictions. Censorship is made up of all restrictions based on one group's idea. Restrictions that are believed by one institute to seem inappropriate, but too many others is something that is not socially needed. Restrictions are not just found in dress code, but in things that affect everyone. From controlled entertainment and musical restrictions to withheld news and banned books, censorship comes to be in anyone's lives whether you are for or against it.

Most if not all people find entertainment in the growing media world. Televisions, radio and even music bring a comforting and resourceful presence to one's life. Movies are not only a source of entertainment, but a topic of conversation between many. Music builds bonds and feelings that can change one person, but music has been censored too. Imagine or remember being thrown back into the year 2001, more specifically September 11, 2001. On this day in the not so past, terrorists hijacked planes and flew them into the Twin Towers in New York City devastating the country. In the days that followed this tragedy our entertainment media was censored. For something so loved by many, music became extensively regulated. Because of potential controversy and potential "hurt," feelings 150+ songs were categorized as questionable and were highly pushed to be restrained on the radio. Things like The Coup's album cover for, "Party Music," was not to be printed because it was of the band standing in front of the burning World Trade Center. The leader of the band, Boots Riley said, "it was supposed to be a metaphor for the capitalist state being destroyed through music," and even though this artwork was created 18 months prior to the attack it was still taken down. Other examples of artist feeling pressured into sensitivity of music censorship during 9/11 include changes in release dates like Dave Matthews's "When the World Ends," single, the Cranberries's music video, "Anylasis," was taken down for repeated images skyscrapers and airplanes and changed lyrics having to do with the police and the possible sensitivity it could bring to people. There are other times in history when music censorship has been shown. Countless songs have been banned at some point due to references to sex, drugs and other related topics. This though, doesn't make sense. Artist have artistic freedom with their music while everyone has music as a freedom. Tom Morello of Rage Against the Machines said about censorship, "[questionable songs] encourage people to question the kind of ignorance that breeds intolerance. Intolerance which can lead to censorship." He went on to say, "[censorship] at it's extremes can lead to the kind of violence we witnessed," when speaking of the 9/11 attack and the music censorship along with it. Music at any time in history, past or present, should not be banned for a singular group's opinion or things that could possibly arise. This not only protects people from things like 9/11, but brings a comfort and enjoyment to many people.

Censorship of entertainment is not just found in music, but in television. Although movies and shows have a rating, it is only a general rating. It is based off a percentage of the population while different people have different levels of maturity. Coming from parent's permission should someone younger be allowed to watch something. A mature teenager or young adult should be allowed to watch a rated R movie with themes like graphic violence, sexual content and hate speech with the consent of a guardian. Movies like PG-13 and R and shows like TV-14 and TV-MA should be available to everyone because each person like having their own sense of style and music likings, have different levels of maturity.

Too each person entertainment is a huge part of their lives, but so is the news they have. Yes, although it may not be known to everyone there are cases of news censorship in the past and present. Since 1791 when the first Amendment in the Bill of Rights was established, the people have had the right to free speech and in some cases more importantly, freedom of press. Although restriction of news to all of the population comes with punishable fines, imprisonments, confiscation, prohibition and or closing of the source, there is still instances of news censorship. For instance in 1942 during WWII, the United States government enforced wartime practices. With bans on weather forecasts that could possibly help enemies in air time attacks and restricted listener requests that could help enemies with communicating with each other through codes, the news was limited. Although this is reasonable it was only the beginning and one of the first instances of media censorship. By denying this news, yes we were preventing the possibility of helping the enemy, but we were taking away the rights of our own U.S. citizens. These securities make the government feel secure, but the citizens clueless. As a democratic nation, the U.S. is reliant on information to make each person feel educated and confident in their votes and decisions. This information can't be given to some and not to other because as the 1st Amendment explains, we have the freedom of press. Different information to only certain people deflates the idea of equal votes with equal information. The Constitution guarantees everyone has equal information along with the freedom to publish information to anyone. Since news matters to everyone there is a set of rules called the Media Ownership Rules that in basic state that one company can't have all or too much power over the news business. Without this, only one viewpoint may be shown by one group instead of both sides of the story. News really matters. Each person needs it too make their best judgement that impact the wellbeing of their future. So why keep information like political and different statistics when they could make your future a home or a hell?

When you think of gathering information you probably think of using the internet, but with censored news it may be hard to trust. Therefore the most reliable source must fall upon books. Censored books though, are yet another restricted topics. Throughout history, books have been the most used form of censorship. Like all other censorship though, it is all based on "what ifs," and possibilities. Most instances of book restrictions are found within religious institutes where topics of books don't directly align with the religion's beliefs. That however doesn't make sense when a book is taken away from everyone because of one powered influence. Concerned parents and unresourceful school employees aim to protect the children they care for when really what they are doing is sheltering the growing kids in this ever changing world. With different moral standards different people have different ideas of rules for different controversial topics in books like profane language, witchcraft, violence, sex, politics and alternate life styles. In this socially developing world books are still banned that have to do with same sex relationships and classic pieces like, "Huckleberry Finn," by Mark Twain because of terms and instances used in a part of history. In the past some U.S. Post Offices refused to ship and bring some books into the country because they didn't match their beliefs. Since then though, courts have ruled multiple times that if books have "dirty words," it doesn't automatically make them dirty or inappropriate. To show these problems the American Library Association hosts Banned Book Week in the last week of September to show support to popular children and adult books that have been challenged or banned.

Like Vermont's governor, Howard Dean, said after the 9//11 attack, "A reevaluation of the importance of some of our specific civil liberties," some protections need to be made to keep everyone safe at all times. Taking away freedom of how one dresses, entertainment, music, news and books won't help everyone. Everyone has different morals and instead of taking away everything from the majority because of one minority, have the minority not use the materials they don't like and keep the things for the majority that make today the 21st century ours.

Citations:

Kimmelman, Gene. *Censorship by Media Conglomerates Threatens Democracy.* U.S. Senate

Committee on Commerce, Science, and Transportation, 2003.

"Censorship." Encyclopedia. World News Digest, Infobase Learning,

http://wnd.infobaselearning.com/recordurl.aspx?wid=152188&nid=4542&umbtype=2. Accessed

2 Oct. 2017.

"Banned Books." *Gale Student REsources in Context,* Gale, 2017.

Nuzum, Eric. "Censorship of Music After September 11 Terrorist Attacks." *Censorship,* edited

by Kate Burns, Greenhaven Press, 2004.

Mrs. Hussey

Physical Science CP

19 January 2017

Should We Say No To Nuclear?

Imagine living your everyday life, when suddenly, an alarm begins blaring and you're forced to evacuate your home and city. A nearby nuclear power plant had just exploded, spreading intense radiation for hundreds of miles, and killing many people in a tragic event. This tragedy was a reality for all of those living near the Chernobyl Nuclear Power Plant in 1986, and something like this is bound to happen again. Currently, "there is around a 50% chance that a major nuclear disaster will occur by 2050" (Wheatly). That amount seems surprisingly high for a method of energy generation that is becoming more widespread every year. Shouldn't our priority be safety? I believe that we should not continue to use nuclear energy as our main source of energy production, if it can be this deadly.

What even is a nuclear power plant? A nuclear power plant generates energy through the process of fission (the splitting of one nucleus into two smaller ones, creating energy). The fuel that most nuclear reactors use is an isotope of uranium, called Uranium-235. Uranium is a very common metal found in the earth in many places, and Uranium-235 must be extracted from the uranium that is found. It is a nonrenewable resource, but will not run out any time soon.

During nuclear fission, a neutron is sent to collide with the Uranium-235, causing it to split into Krypton-92, Barium-141 and more neutrons, as well as releasing heat and radiation.

The radiation that this process emits can alter and destroy parts of our DNA, possibly causing gene mutation and other damage, which can lead to cancers. These neutrons that were released then go on to split more atoms of Uranium-235, causing a chain reaction which creates the energy in a nuclear power plant. The energy created boils water nearby and causes it to spin a turbine, creating the energy that we receive. The Krypton-92 and Barium-141 that are leftover become radioactive waste, which remains radioactive for many years, which is stored in a safe environment for the duration of its half-life, and is then disposed of.

Because of all of the possible risks that come from operating a nuclear power plant creating tremendous amounts of energy and radiation, there are many places where something can go disastrously wrong. There are many times where something has gone wrong in a nuclear power plant, and in a few, more extreme cases, the accident resulted in casualties. Some of the most catastrophic events in human history were the disasters in Chernobyl and Fukushima (two famous nuclear power plant disasters). As stated by Rose Kivi, in the area of Chernobyl, a total of 30 people were killed within four months of when the plant's reactors was destroyed, and many others were killed because of cancer caused by the radiation released from the plant (Kivi). How could something like this have ever happened?

There are so many potential places where something devastating could happen in a nuclear power plant. They can be very dependant on outside forces and electricity/power, since the entire process of the nuclear fission must be contained at a certain temperature. Without electricity, it could overheat, and many natural disasters could entirely destroy a power plant. Also, there is the possibility that small acts of human error would have tremendous results. It is definitive dangerous risk to run nuclear power plants around large communities, but yet people still choose to do so. There's also quite a high probability that a dangerous nuclear meltdown like Fukushima, or even worse, could happen again in the coming years. According to Dr. Good Heart, the NRC (Nuclear Regulatory Commission), has stated that the odds of another catastrophic event is 1 in a million years, although, after the incident at Fukushima, Japan has begun claiming that the likelihood is currently 1 in 40 years (Dr. Good Heart). Obviously, someone doesn't have their facts straight. But still, if people are beginning to claim that there is a significant chance that a disaster could happen again, then is it worth continuing to use nuclear energy if we are effectively putting many people's lives at risk?

There are many other alternatives to nuclear energy, and many of which are much safer. There are many types of renewable energy that we can easily utilize, while the uranium in the power plants will eventually run out, but not for a very long time, since there is an abundant supply. Energy sources such as solar panels, wind turbines, and hydropower, while having high investment costs, can make up for the initial costs, and much more, while being a much safer alternative to nuclear power. They all can produce decent amounts of energy, which can possibly become more cost effective than nuclear energy, because of all the safety precautions and other expenses that must be paid for. Nuclear power can end up costing much, much, more, because of all regulations and the costs of all of the components, so it can seem fairly ineffective to use nuclear power instead of other sources ("Energy Source Comparison"). Would you want to end up paying more in your taxes for a power source that can be less effective than "green" energy sources, which you may even be using at your own home? Also, many countries have started using more and more renewable energy sources such as solar power, with Germany, Italy, Belgium, and the Czech Republic at the top of the list ("Alternative Energy Sources"). If many other countries are utilizing these other sources of power more, then it obviously is not a terrible idea to do so as well.

There are many arguments that someone could make for using nuclear power instead of renewable power sources. Some people may argue that nuclear power is more efficient and can provide more energy than other power sources. Also, they can create many more job opportunities than other energy sources, which can reduce unemployment rates and help families receive a better income. However, would you want to risk these new worker's lives for more power? No matter how much people try to reduce the dangers of nuclear power, there is still a chance that an accident will happen and lead to more deaths in the future. Also, nuclear power produces no $CO_2$ or greenhouse gases, so it can be argued that it is better for the environment. However, nuclear power produces much radioactive waste that is stored in the environment, which can have various dangerous health effects and effects on the environment itself, which can be very detrimental. There are still many types of renewable energy sources like solar power and wind energy that produce no greenhouse gases and are much safer as well.

All of the changes from nuclear power to more natural, renewable energy would have a tremendous impact on the future of America. To begin with, the switch could cost trillions of dollars over a span of 20 years ("A Renewable World: What Will It Cost?"). It would put the U.S even further into debt, and would take a very long time to complete the transition, and would be very inefficient as well. However, making the switch to all renewable energy would "virtually eliminate air pollution, thus avoiding health costs to the tune of $600 billion a year by 2050. Meanwhile, moving everything to carbon-free electricity would avoid about $3.3 trillion a year in global climate change costs of US emissions by 2050" (Roberts). While we would be getting money back, and it will eventually balance out, it still would be very difficult. While I think we should use nuclear power less, I do not believe that we should switch solely to "green" energy sources, as it is just frankly unrealistic.

Works Cited

"Alternative Energy Sources." *Science in Context*, Gale Cengage Learning, 2011,

http://link.galegroup.com/apps/doc/CV2644150058/SCIC?u=nhais_hdpm&xid=4da7a8a0.

"A Renewable World: What Will It Cost?" *Knowledge@Wharton*, Wharton University, 23 Apr.

2015, knowledge.wharton.upenn.edu/article/a-renewable-world-what-will-it-cost/.

Dr. Good Heart. "What Is The Statistical Probability, What Are The Odds Of A Major Nuclear

Accident Like Fukushima In The USA Or In Your Country?" *A Green Road Journal*, 2 July

2017, www.agreenroadjournal.com/2013/09/what-is-statistical-probability-of.html.

"Energy Source Comparison." *energy4me Energy Source Comparison Comments*,

energy4me.org/all-about-energy/what-is-energy/energy-sources/.

Kivi, Rose. "Nuclear Energy Disasters Are Inevitable." *Opposing Viewpoints in Context*, Gale

Cengage Learning, 2010,

http://link.galegroup.com/apps/doc/EJ3010706209/OVIC?u=nhais_hdpm&xid=1cd7b91f.

Roberts, David. "Here's what it would take for the US to run on 100% renewable energy." *Vox*,

Vox Media, 9 June 2015, www.vox.com/2015/6/9/8748081/us-100-percent-renewable-energy.

Wheatley, Spencer, et al. "Of Disasters and Dragon Kings: A Statistical Analysis of Nuclear Power Incidents & Accidents." *ArXiv*, Cornell University Library, 7 Apr. 2015, arxiv.org/abs/1504.02380.

# ↑ *A Thin Line* ↓

An in depth writing piece on genocide and humanity in our world wide society today

---

5/23/17

Dear reader,

    When we started this project, I was told to find a research topic. It had to be something that interests me, something that I could write four genre pieces on. Like any other student I started aimlessly searching the web by searching things that I was interested in. None of these things had something that I felt was worth writing about. They had nothing I could write on and on about for four whole genres. I like to dance but this doesn't mean the history of dance interests me, it's the actual moment that is enjoyable, not merely the idea of it or how it came to be. I had a tough couple of research days, I found nothing. I decided that I needed to finally get something solid that I could write on. So, I went to New York Times website and scrolled until I found something that evoked some type of response from me. I found a video.

    There was a journalistic expository video on a situation in the Philippines titled "When a president says 'I'll kill you.' " This intrigued me. It showed the people of the country and how this wide spread drug issue was affecting them but most had a larger issue. It was how the president was handling it. The video showed graphic images of people dead and it wasn't due to overdose, they were murdered by their own president. He'd given a speech saying that they need to kill anyone involved in drugs and his people listened.

    After watching this video I decided I wanted to learn more about it because what was going on reminded me of something we recently learned about in world history, genocide. The leader was just killing people off and I thought, "this is something worth writing about." I thought it was something that should be in the papers, a genocide in the making is how I was looking at it. I found many articles talking about this current event, some explaining the president's stance and others telling horror stories of loved ones lost for being in the wrong place at the wrong time.

    The four genres I've picked to write about this are, a recipe, journal entrees, a poem, and an editorial. I chose the poem to showcase and explain what a genocide is and how it begins. I wrote the journal entrees to show the perspective of the president as well as someone who supports him. I wrote the poem to show these two conflicting arguments and perspectives for the reader to see and explore this topic. And I wrote the editorial to bring all my points together, to show my stance on the topic, and to work in as much information as possible while connecting the two main ideas on my project. That there is a thin line between drug control and genocide.

*Love the Questions: Reclaiming Research with Curiosity and Passion* by Cathy Fraser.
Copyright © 2018. Stenhouse Publishers.

*A Recipe For Genocide with Ten Simple Ingredients*

❖   1 cup of **classification**

❖   ½ cup of **symbolization**

❖   2 cups of **discrimination**

❖   A sprinkle of **dehumanization**

❖   A generous amount of **organization**

❖   Two whole sticks of **polarization**

❖   ⅔ cup of fresh **preparation**

❖   Fill two bowls almost to the brim with **persecution**

❖   A large amount (5 cups) of **extermination**

❖   3 cups of **denial**

*Instructions*

❖ Take the **classification** and pour it into a society, this should separate into two groups, "us and them".

❖ Next add in the **symbolization,** this will classify the ingredients further to help separate mixtures.

❖ Then add in your two cups of **discrimination**, this will insure that there are laws in place to separate mixtures.

❖ Once you've done this sprinkle in some **dehumanization** and make sure it is evenly distributed throughout, this will dehumanize the lower class from the higher.

❖ Add a generous amount of **organization** into a separate bowl, as this will act as a base.

❖ After this add one whole stick of **polarization** into each bowl to give the mixture some scare tactics.

❖ Chop up some fresh **preparation** and mix that in to ready the mixture to be baked.

❖ Fill each bowl almost to the brim with **persecution** as you slowly mix in a large amount of **extermination,** this will start to take care of the majority of your baking "problems".

❖ Continue to combine the two mixtures together and pour it into a pan. After that, coat the top with a thick layer of **denial** to cover up what you've done. Carefully place in oven and bake for 45 minutes or until completely gone.

## *Senselessness*

It needs to stop.

IT NEEDS TO STOP
ALL THESE DRUGS

All this killing, it's too much

YOU NEED TO UNDERSTAND, IT'S PLAGUING OUR COUNTRY

I guess I understood at first but not now

IT SHOULD BE PUT TO AN END

They took my brother,
He didn't deserve that.

He was an innocent man

NONE OF THEM ARE INNOCENT

He slipped up once

THEY KNOW WHAT THEY ARE GETTING INTO

And it cost him his life

IT IS THEIR LIFE THEY RISK

This is senseless.

THEY ARE SENSELESS.

11/16/2016

Dear Journal,

The Philippines recently elected our new president, Rodrigo Duterte. I'm glad about this, I did vote for him after all. I think most of his voters stand with him because of his plan on how to control the drug problem we are having here. So many of our good people are turned into villains when these drugs grab hold of their lives. Duterte thinks if we rid them all of our country this epidemic will disappear with them. I guess that makes sense. Good riddance I say, they are only worsening our country.

— Estaban

11/28/16

Dear Journal,

Tonight I watched President Duterte's speech on the tv. It was so inspiring! One of my favorite phrases from the speech was "All of you who are into drugs, you sons of bitches, I will really kill you," No kidding. Once I heard, when he was mayor of one of the cities here in the Philippines, he actually did kill one of the druggies. I think I could pull that off, I always kind of felt that rage toward them, and now it's legal. There's something I could do for my country, I think I'll give it a Shot. Ha.

—Estaban

11/29/16

Dear Journal,

I've started thinking more about what Duterte has been saying and I realize how right he really is. I need to get in on this. For my country! Tomorrow night I'm Gonna go out and get rid of some of these rock bottom druggies, doing nothing for this country except making us all look like addict bums. They make us look crazy. It's time to fight fire with fire. Next time you hear from me I'll be a changed man.

                    -Estaban

11/30/16

Dear Journal,

Last night I made my first ever kill. It was a strange feeling, but not a bad one. They do deserve it after all. President Duterte would be proud. I am a little nervous about getting caught though. If I were to be caught I think the President would eventually get me out. He knows that many of us are trying to live out his dream for our community, just getting rid of the worst parts of it. He said in one of his speeches that anyone arrested for this would get out if he had anything to do with it. What a good president.

                    -Estaban

12/5/16

Dear journal,

It's been a good week. Ten of these drugs rats killed tonight and four of them by me. I've joined a group of others, like myself, that want to carry out Duterte's vision for the Philippines. We call ourselves the pistols of justice. We go out almost every night to find as many of the heathens as we can and put them to their well deserved deaths. It's a breeze now, killing them. My conscience is as clear as day, there is no doubt that all these people deserve what they are getting. They put themselves in this position and now the cold hand of justice will slap them in the face.

              –Estaban

# A thin line

It is 2017. People are dying, and not all of them should be. As a society, we have come along way. But in certain contexts I believe we are mistaking the amount of human progress we've made. We are so far from this goal of world peace, individual countries can't even manage such a level of harmony. There are places  and leaders in this world doing awful things, conducting acts of violence, and it's because they believe it is what's right. That it will work.

The topic of genocide is a tough and sensitive one. The holocaust, being one of the most famous of these many heart wrenching events, was especially awful. Millions of innocent people being killed purely for their religion and status in society. Violence is not the right path to peace, I'm not here to tell you what that is, because I sure as hell don't know, but I do know what it isn't. Peace is not fighting, peace is not violence, peace is definitely not killing and killing is not a problem solver.

President Duterte, the Philippine's newest leader believes otherwise. He is taking this path of violence in a very extreme way, almost like anarchy. He has been promoting the killing of anyone who is involved in drugs at all. Does this make sense? I mean if he kills them all there goes your drug problem, right? I'm not so sure. Of course I understand drugs are not something we want being used so heavily. They have bad effects on a community and on an individual. There are few issues that are slightly outlying in this plan. Number one: if all the druggies are gone, it's very, *very* likely that new ones will develop again, addiction is a disease. Number two: *This Is killing off a whole population  within a community.* Is that not enough? Is it still a good idea? Believe it or not many citizens of the Philippines think so.

We as Americans might think this is a low point, barbaric even. But if we're being honest it's not that far fetched. A new way to deal with the drug problem we're having! A good amount of us would probably be ecstatic "Kill 'em all!", "Those bastards made a choice." Which they did. They made an awful life ruining choice and it was stupid, that's punishable, but not by death. After this choice though, most addicts, eventually want to go back. But no, they can't. It's almost always too late. They're addicted.

Addiction is something that happens in the brain and affects the nervous system, like the release of dopamine and amount and dopamine receptors. When they take the drugs an insane amount of dopamine is released, so to compensate some of the dopamine receptors don't function anymore. This way, if they aren't taking drugs, things that would normally make this person happy (by releasing dopamine), wouldn't compare to the amount of pleasure they'd receive when doing drugs. With that, the receptors are no longer as sensitive.

President duterte definitely does not understand this, It's still something we are trying to understand here is America. Addiction can't be solved by incarceration, and especially not by killing all addicts off. It takes time, treatment, and people who care. Not mass amounts of violence and killing. It is now reaching a point where 5 to over 13 people are being killed a night , because they, allegedly, were involved with drugs.

People in the philippines and around the world need to realize that incarceration and death are certainly not the answers to this widespread drug problem we are having. There are actually people and governments in this world tha decided just killing these people, these people with families and lives, they've just been wiped from the planet with no chance to renew. Do we realize what we are doing to these people that need such a substantial amount of help? Do we know what they go through every day trying to get off of this stuff? Do we see it, that line that we've begun to cross? That is the thin line between a drug control problem, no, a drug epidemic and a genocide in the works.

# Endnotes

### 1. *"A Recipe for Genocide in Ten Simple Steps"*

In this piece I am trying to introduce the reader to what the word genocide means and how something so drastic starts. I used the ingredient list to show all of the components needed for this and then a separate instruction page that shows each step and explains what it is or how it's executed. I chose a recipe as a genre because it takes a shadowy topic and gives it a more sarcastic and casual tone, I think this made it easier to explain as well as easier for the reader to understand.

### 2. *"Senselessness"*

My second piece is a poem. I wrote this piece to show and introduce two differing perspectives on drug control and how it is handled in certain places. It is a two voice poem with a voice of a family member or close relative of someone involved in drugs speaking with someone in a government stance like an official or president. I think this shows these two conflicting perspectives and could be more focused on the situation in the philippines with people being killed nightly with the drug control approach of the government. Although this piece is short I think it contributes a lot to my overall point in this project.

### 3. *"Dear Journal"*

In my third piece I used journal entries in a first person perspective to show the opinions and values of someone supporting President Duterte and well as the opinion of the president himself. I wanted to present an opposing argument in a non-bias way while also still conveying that this is something I do not agree with. I tried to do this using a slightly extreme and sarcastic tone like I had in other pieces.

### 4. *"A thin line"*

My fourth piece, I think, is one of my strongest. I wanted it to show all aspects of my project to weave all of the separate ideas together. I wanted it to include argument from two sides as well as showing my opinion I. I also wanted to add some factual aspects to it. Over all I wanted this piece to bring home my main points and still keep the slightly sarcastic tonality that I've been taking with most of my pieces for my arguments.

# Annotated Bibliography

*When a President Says 'I'll Kill You''*. Dir. Andrew Glazer and Jeremy Rocklin. *New York Times*. New York Times, n.d. Web. 11 Apr. 2017.

This Source was the one that truly got my project started. I found it while scrolling through the New York Times website and the title really interested me, "When a President Says 'I'll Kill You'." It was a video including the president of the philippines giving a brute speech to a room of professionals telling how anyone involved with drugs should be rid of *HIS* country- killed off. It showed graphic images of people who have been claimed by this effort of his war on drugs. Their loved ones were showed crying hysterically above them, being pushed away by the police. "Why are you here, Lito? You were just alive!" One of the girls screamed this and it sped my heart rate. I had found something worth writing about. It was a journalistic and expository video to show what was going on in the philippines. It gave me a lot of inspiration as well as helpful information for my research. It showed me what was happening in this other part of the world and how that could affect so many people.

Stanton, Gregory H. "Ten Stages of Genocide." *Genocide Education Project*. The Genocide Education Project, n.d. Web. 11 Apr. 2017.

I got this source from my world history class a month or two ago. We were learning about genocides around the world like the Holocaust and the Rwandan genocide. The article is basically a formula for how a society can engage in genocide. It goes through the ten stages that have shown to be common themes in all genocides and dissects and explains what they mean and how it happens. When I was doing my research about what was happening In the Philippines, I started to recognize some of the signs and themes of a genocide. I looked more into this article after that and it gave me lots of useful information to help guide my writing. It helped me make accurate points about my topic with a source to back up my statements and observations.

Iyengar, Rishi, et al. "The Killing Season inside Philippine President Rodrigo Duterte's War on Drugs." *Time*, vol. 188, no. 14, 10 Oct. 2016, pp. 46-49. EBSCO*host*, search.ebscohost.com/login.aspx?direct=true&db=aph&AN=118457516&site=ehost-live.

I found this source kind of in the middle of my research and It seemed like just what I was looking for. It discussed what was going on in the Philippines from a journalistic point of view. It went into details of arguments from both points of view using quotes and such. This gave a political perspective but most likely in a bias way, they pulled quotes from speeches Duterte had given as well as some from people who support him. It showed how a lot of Filipinos support his actions and think that what he is doing is right and truly the best option. It also gave many statistics that I think really helped me in digging into this topic further and kept me wanting to learn more. It also made me realize that a lot of others saw this as a problem, but no one yet had even begun to compare it to a genocide and that's what made me really want to write this. It is a piece to put it out there that this is what I think and how i'm perceiving it, even if it doesn't leave the english classroom.

Santos, Ana P. "A Philippine Senator Defies Her President - from behind Bars." *Los Angeles Times,*
Los Angeles Times,
www.latimes.com/world/asia/la-fg-philippines-delima-20170326-story.html. Accessed 25 May
2017.

My last two sources are very similar to my third in the sense that all three are journalistic pieces. All go
over the same topic and have pretty much the same argument, but each of them added something
original and new to my piece. This article starts showing the reader what kind of person President Duterte
is. It gives an example of a local senator that called for an investigation into his bloody drug "solution". He
responded with many forms of violence from verbal threats to make her cry to promises to throw her and
jail and destroy her. After such an introduction the piece explains further what the recently elected leader
had been doing and how it is affecting individuals lives in the Philippines.This article really helped me to
get that perspective and build on my pieces that include voices from individuals like that.

Jenkins, Nash. "Death Reigns on the Streets of Duterte's Philippines." *Time,* vol. 189, no. 3, 16 Jan.
2017, pp. 28-37. EBSCO*host,*
search.ebscohost.com/login.aspx?direct=true&db=aph&AN=120565248&site=ehost-live.

This is one of my most recent sources. It focuses on the conditions of the Philippines as of 2017. It is
almost the same thing as "The Killing season" but this source has the newest updates on things like death
tolls and how the government is continuing to function in the country. This is also one of my shorter
sources but It still had a lot to offer and contributed to my piece. It also talks about life in the slums of the
Philippines, where drugs seem to be a bigger issue. It helped me form my voice not only for a victim of
this situation but also a supporter. All of these people are coming from the same places under very similar
conditions but have such varying views on this conflict. This article helped my understand that more fully
and helped me to try and recreate the variety.

# Bibliography

Alda, Alan. 2017. *If I Understood You, Would I Have This Look on My Face? My Adventures in the Art and Science of Relating and Communicating.* New York: Random House.

Association of College and Research Libraries. 2015. "Framework for Information Literacy for Higher Education." American Library Association, February 2. www.ala.org/acrl/sites/ala.org.acrl/files/content/issues/infolit/Framework_ILHE.pdf.

Ballenger, Bruce. 2015. *The Curious Researcher: A Guide to Writing Research Papers.* 8th ed. Boston: Pearson.

Bauerline, Mark. 2008. *The Dumbest Generation: How the Digital Age Stupefies Young Americans and Jeopardizes Our Future [or, Don't Trust Anyone Under 30].* New York: Penguin.

Beers, Kylene, and Robert E. Probst. 2016. *Reading Nonfiction: Notice & Note Stances, Signposts, and Strategies.* Portsmouth, NH: Heinemann.

Berdik, Chris. 2002. "Duped! When Journalists Fall for Fake News." *Quill*, May 1. https://quill.spjnetwork.org/2002/05/01/Duped-when-journalists-fall-for-fake-news/.

*The Big Bang Theory.* 2008. "The Bath Item Gift Hypothesis." Season 2, episode 11. Burbank, CA: Warner Bros. Television.

Black, Brian. 2006. "Muckrakers and Yellow Journalism." In *American History Through Literature, Volume 2,* ed. Tom Quirk and Gary Schamhorst. Detroit, MI: Charles Scribner's Sons.

Blakely, George T. 1997. "Breathing New Life into Research Papers." *College Teaching* 45 (1): 3.

Bleiberg, Edward I., James Allan Edward, Kristen Mossler Figg, Philip M. Soergel, and John Black Friedman, eds. 2005. "Scholasticism in the Later Middle Ages." *Arts and Humanities Through the Eras, Volume 4: Renaissance Europe 1300–1600.* Detroit, MI: Gale.

Butler, Rebecca P. 2011. *Copyright for Teachers and Librarians in the 21st Century.* New York: Neal-Schuman.

Coffin, Caroline. 2006. *Historical Discourse: The Language of Time, Cause and Evaluation.* London: Continuum. Quoted in Fang, Zhihui, and Mary Schleppegrell. 2008. *Reading in Secondary Content Areas: A Language-Based Pedagogy.* Ann Arbor: University of Michigan Press.

Courier Editorial Staff. 2015. "The Dangers of the Selfie." Sample Editorials, September 20. www.readwritethink.org/files/resources/SampleEditorials.pdf.

Cox, John Woodrow, Theresa Vargas, and Justin W. Moyer. 2018. "He Saw a Dazed Woman Put Out in the Cold by a Baltimore Hospital. He Started Filming." Washington Post, January 12. https://www.washingtonpost.com/local/social-media-fury-follows-video-of-dazed-woman-put-out-in-cold-by-baltimore-hospital/2018/01/11/b8a7866c-f70d-11e7-b34a-b85626af34ef_story.html?utm_term=.b947fbe375f0.

Crutcher, Chris. 2007. Deadline. New York: Greenwillow Books.

Cunningham, Anne E., and Keith E. Stanovich. 1998. "What Reading Does for the Mind." American Educator 22 (1): 8–15.

Desilver, Drew. 2016. "Jobs Requiring Preparation, Social Skills or Both Expected to Grow Most." Pew Research Center, October 13. www.pewresearch.org/fact-tank/2016/10/13/jobs-requiring-preparation-social-skills-or-both-expected-to-grow-most/.

Dugan, Molly A. 2008. "Journalism Ethics and the Independent Journalist." McGeorge Law Review 39 (3): 801–811. www.mcgeorge.edu/Documents/Publications/09_Dugan_MasterMLR39.pdf.

Dweck, Carol S. 2006. Mindset: The New Psychology of Success. New York: Ballantine.

Eco, Umberto. 2015. How to Write a Thesis. Cambridge, MA: The MIT Press.

Eisenberg, Michael, and Robert Berkowitz. 2000. Teaching Information & Technology Skills: The Big6 in Secondary Schools. Worthington, OH: Linworth.

Elbow, Peter, and Pat Belanoff. 1989. Sharing and Responding. New York: Random House.

Erspamer, Francesco. 2015. Foreword to How to Write a Thesis, by Umberto Eco, ix–xiv. Cambridge, MA: The MIT Press.

Fang, Zhihui, and Barbara G. Pace. 2013. "Teaching with Challenging Texts in the Disciplines: Text Complexity and Close Reading." Journal of Adolescent & Adult Literacy 57 (2): 104–108.

Fang, Zhihui, and Mary J. Schleppegrell. 2008. Reading in Secondary Content Areas: A Language-Based Pedagogy. Ann Arbor: University of Michigan Press.

———. 2010. "Disciplinary Literacies Across Content Areas: Supporting Secondary Reading Through Functional Language Analysis." Journal of Adolescent & Adult Literacy 53 (7): 587–597.

Fletcher, Jennifer. 2015. Teaching Arguments: Rhetorical Comprehension, Critique, and Response. Portland, ME: Stenhouse.

Fraser, Cathy, Scott Lasley, and Leah Damien Williams. 2016. "'Ugh Gross': Student Perceptions of Themselves as Researchers." Presentation at the 2016 Annual Convention of the National Council of Teachers of English, Atlanta, Georgia, November 17–20.

Freedman, David H. 2017. "A Reality Check for IBM's AI Ambitions." *MIT Technology Review*, June 27. https://www.technologyreview.com/s/607965/a-reality-check-for-ibms-ai-ambitions/.

Frey, Nancy, and Douglas Fisher. 2013. *Rigorous Reading: 5 Access Points for Comprehending Complex Texts.* Thousand Oaks, CA: Corwin.

Friedman, Thomas L. 2016. *Thank You for Being Late: An Optimist's Guide to Thriving in the Age of Accelerations.* New York: Farrar, Straus and Giroux.

Gallagher, Kelly. 2006. *Teaching Adolescent Writers.* Portland, ME: Stenhouse.

———. 2011. *Write Like This: Teaching Real-World Writing Through Modeling & Mentor Texts.* Portland, ME: Stenhouse.

———. 2015. *In the Best Interest of Students: Staying True to What Works in the ELA Classroom.* Portland, ME: Stenhouse.

Gardner, Eriq. 2017. "Conan O'Brien Headed to Trial Over Claims of Stealing Jokes." *The Hollywood Reporter*, May 15. https://www.hollywoodreporter.com/thr-esq/conan-obrien-headed-trial-claims-stealing-jokes-1003727.

Gardner, Walt. 2010. "Student Responsibility for Learning." *Education Week* blog, May 19. http://blogs.edweek.org/edweek/walt_gardners_reality_check/2010/05/student_responsibility_for_learning.html.

Gasaway, Lolly. 2003. "When U.S. Works Pass into the Public Domain." University of North Carolina. https://www.unc.edu/~unclng/public-d.htm.

Gasparyan, Diana. 2016. "Artificial Intelligence and Semantics Through the Prism of Structural, Post-Structural and Transcendental Approaches." *Integrative Psychological & Behavioral Science* 50 (4): 701–743.

Gerber, Hannah R., Sandra Schramroth Abrams, Jen Scott Curwood, and Alecia Marie Magnifico. 2017. *Conducting Qualitative Research of Learning in Online Spaces.* Los Angeles: Sage.

Graves, Donald H. 1984. *A Researcher Learns to Write: Selected Articles and Monographs.* Exeter, NH: Heinemann.

Hacker, Diana, and Nancy Somers. 2015. *A Pocket Style Manual.* 7th ed. Boston: Bedford St. Martin's.

Hassett, Kevin A., and Michael R. Strain. 2016. "Expect 25 Years of Rapid Change." *Monthly Labor Review*, US Bureau of Labor Statistics, March.

Herold, Benjamin. 2014. "Digital Reading Poses Learning Challenges for Students." *Education Week* 33 (1): 24–25.

Hillocks Jr., George. 2011. *Teaching Argument Writing, Grades 6–12: Supporting Claims with Relevant Evidence and Clear Reasoning.* Portsmouth, NH: Heinemann.

Hooley, Diana S., Lee Ann Tysseling, and Beverly Ray. 2013. "Trapped in a Cycle of Low Expectations: An Exploration of High School Seniors' Perspectives About Academic Reading." *High School Journal* 96 (4): 321–328.

Jabr, Ferris. 2013. "Why the Brain Prefers Paper." *Scientific American* 309 (5): 48.

Krathwohl, David R. 2002. "A Revision of Bloom's Taxonomy: An Overview." *Theory into Practice* 41 (4): 212–218.

Kuhlthau, Carol C., Leslie K. Maniotes, and Ann K. Caspari. 2012. *Guided Inquiry Design: A Framework for Inquiry in Your School.* Santa Barbara, CA: Libraries Unlimited.

Labaree, David. 2018. "The Five-Paragraph Fetish." aeon, February 15. https://aeon.co/essays/writing-essays-by-formula-teaches-students-how-to-not-think.

Lasley, Scott, Cathy Fraser, and Leah Damien Williams. Submitted. "Developing a Palate: The Value of Student Choice and Investment in Research Writing."

Leko, Melinda M., and Charlotte A. Mundy. 2012. "Preparing Secondary Educators to Support Adolescent Struggling Readers." *Preventing School Failure* 56 (2): 137–147.

Lent, Releah Cossett. 2015. *This Is Disciplinary Literacy: Reading, Writing, Thinking, and Doing . . . Content Area by Content Area.* Thousand Oaks, CA: Corwin.

MacLeod, Don. 2012. *How to Find Out Anything: From Extreme Google Searches to Scouring Government Documents, A Guide to Uncovering Anything About Everyone and Everything.* New York: Prentice Hall.

Maehre, Jeff. 2009. "What It Means to Ban Wikipedia." *College Teaching* 57 (4): 229–236.

Massachusetts Institute of Technology. n.d. "What Is Common Knowledge?" *Academic Integrity at MIT: A Handbook for Students.* https://integrity.mit.edu/handbook/citing-your-sources/what-common-knowledge.

McDaniel, Kathryn N. 2014. "Read Long and Prosper: Five Do's and Don'ts for Preparing Students for College." *Clearing House: A Journal of Educational Strategies Issues and Ideas* 87 (2): 83–87.

Miller, N. Warren, and Marie E. Lassmann. 2013. "What Are We Teaching Our Students?" *Education* 134 (2): 167–171.

Modern Language Association of America. 2016. *MLA Handbook.* 8th ed. New York: Modern Language Association.

Newkirk, Thomas, and Lisa C. Miller, eds. 2009. *The Essential Don Murray: Lessons from America's Greatest Writing Teacher.* Portsmouth, NH: Heinemann.

Nichols, Sharon L., and David C. Berliner. 2008. "Testing the Joy Out of Learning." *Educational Leadership* 65 (6): 14–18.

O'Connor, Lisa, Melissa Bowles-Terry, Erin Davis, and Wendy Holliday. 2010. "Writing Information Literacy: Revisited Application of Theory to Practice in the Classroom." *Reference & User Services Quarterly* 49 (3): 225–230.

Paige, David D., Timothy V. Rasinski, and Theresa Magpuri-Lavell. 2012. "Is Fluent, Expressive Reading Important for High School Readers?" *Journal of Adolescent & Adult Literacy* 56 (1): 67–76.

The Pell Institute. 2017. "Analyze Qualitative Data." *Evaluation Toolkit.* http://toolkit.pellinstitute.org/evaluation-guide/analyze/analyze-qualitative-data/.

Polk, Tracy, Melissa P. Johnston, and Stephanie Evers. 2015. "Wikipedia Use in Research: Perceptions in Secondary Schools." *Techtrends: Linking Research and Practice to Improve Learning* 59 (3): 92–102.

Purcell, Kristen, Lee Rainie, Alan Heaps, Judy Buchanan, Linda Friedrich, Amanda Jacklin, Clara Chen, and Kathryn Zickuhr. 2012. *How Teens Do Research in the Digital World.* Pew Research Center. http://pewinternet.org/2012/11/01/how-teens-do-research-in-the-digital-world/.

Putz, Melinda. 2006. *A Teacher's Guide to the Multigenre Research Project: Everything You Need to Get Started.* Portsmouth, NH: Heinemann.

Reeves, Douglas B. 2010. *Transforming Professional Development into Student Results.* Alexandria, VA: ASCD.

Rief, Linda. 2014. *Read Write Teach: Choice and Challenge in the Reading-Writing Workshop.* Portsmouth, NH: Heinemann.

Romano, Tom. 2000. *Blending Genre, Altering Style: Writing Multigenre Papers.* Portsmouth, NH: Heinemann.

Rosenblatt, Louise M. 1995. *Literature as Exploration.* 5th ed. New York: Modern Language Association.

Rosenwasser, David, and Jill Stephen. 2008. *Writing Analytically with Readings.* Boston: Thompson.

Seroff, Jole. 2015. "Developing a Curriculum in Intellectual Freedom: What Our Students Need to Know." *Knowledge Quest* 44 (1): 20–24.

Shanahan, Timothy, and Cynthia Shanahan. 2008. "Teaching Disciplinary Literacy to Adolescents: Rethinking Content-Area Literacy." *Harvard Educational Review* 78 (1): 40–59.

Society of Professional Journalists. 1996. "SPJ Code of Ethics." https://spj.org/pdf/spj-code-of-ethics.pdf.

Stanford History Education Group. 2016. "Executive Summary. Evaluating Information: The Cornerstone of Civic Online Reasoning." Stanford University, November 22. https://stacks.stanford.edu/file/druid:fv751yt5934/SHEG%20Evaluating%20Information%20Online.pdf.

*Star Trek: The Next Generation.* 1991. "In Theory." Season 4, episode 25. Los Angeles: Paramount.

Sullenberger III, Chesley B., and Jeffrey Zaslow. 2009. *Sully: My Search for What Really Matters.* New York: William Morrow.

Sydell, Laura. 2016. "We Tracked Down a Fake News Creator in the Suburbs. Here's What We Learned." *All Things Considered,* November 23. https://www.npr.org/sections/alltechconsidered/2016/11/23/503146770/npr-finds-the-head-of-a-covert-fake-news-operation-in-the-suburbs.

Tovani, Cris. 2004. *Do I Really Have to Teach Reading? Content Comprehension, Grades 6–12*. Portland, ME: Stenhouse.

University of Leicester. n.d. "Module 9: Introduction to Research: 3. "The Ten Steps of Content Analysis." https://www.le.ac.uk/oerresources/lill/fdmvco/module9/page_74.htm.

Wiggins, Grant, and Jay McTighe. 2005. *Understanding by Design*. 2nd ed. Alexandria, VA: ASCD.

Wilhelm, Jeffrey D., and Michael W. Smith. 2017. *Diving Deep into Nonfiction: Transferable Tools for Reading ANY Nonfiction Text, Grades 6–12*. Thousand Oaks, CA: Corwin.

Wilkins, Chuck, Eric Rolfhus, Jennifer Hartman, Sarah Brasiel, Jessica Brite, Noel Howland, and Regional Educational Laboratory Southwest. 2012. "How Prepared Are Subgroups of Texas Students for College-Level Reading? Applying a Lexile-Based Approach." REL Technical Brief No. 018.

Wineburg, Sam. 2001. *Historical Thinking and Other Unnatural Acts: Charting the Future of Teaching the Past*. Philadelphia: Temple University Press.

# Index

Page numbers followed by *f* indicate figures.